Pavilions for Giving

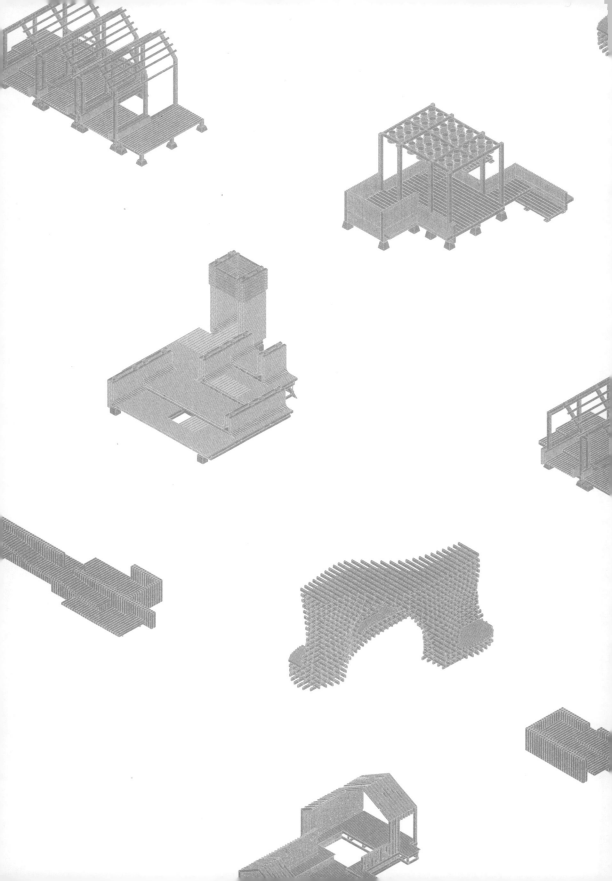

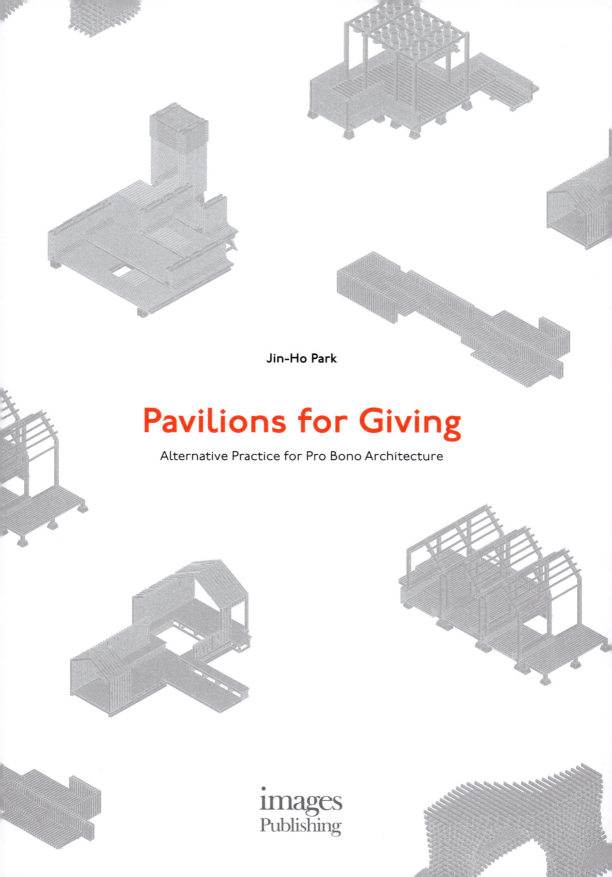

Jin-Ho Park

Pavilions for Giving

Alternative Practice for Pro Bono Architecture

images
Publishing

"Without doubt the individualistic, art-for-art's sake view of the aesthete has been successfully challenged by a generation of architects who are developing a set of standards focused on contemporary social conceptions, and who have therefore joined hands with the professional planners. I have always taken an active part in this movement, and now we have before us the unique opportunity of putting these new standards to their practical tests."

Walter Gropius

Rebuilding our Communities, Chicago: id Book, 1945, p.13.

Contents

8   **Foreword**
by Mark Mack

10   **Introduction**
by Jin-Ho Park

Six Works

36   Street Pavilion

60   Courtyard Hideout

84   Cascading Grounds

112   Blooming Landscape

140   Bucket Pavilion

164   Seoksu Community Pavilion

186   **Interview**
by Design Research and Innovation Laboratory

191   **Acknowledgments**

Foreword

I have known Jin-Ho since the early nineties, when he was working on his PhD on Rudolph Michael Schindler at the University of California, Los Angeles (UCLA) . He impressed me with his academic seriousness and his emergence into a theme that must have been very alien for him, since his culture and his schooling in Korea could not prepare him for the idiosyncrasies of the post-Habsburg Viennese culture out of which Schindler emerged.

I had just arrived at UCLA after teaching at the University of California, Berkeley and had become involved with the iconic Schindler House as a board member for the MAK Center and remain a frequent contributor to the various activities there. I believe that Jin-Ho's fascination with this Austrian architect was based on the rationality inherent in his architectural projects, especially the Schindler Frame on which Jin-Ho based his research and focus.[1] That project prescribes a consistent way of building technology that included local traditions. Timber construction, climatic freedom, inside/outside living in California, and social economics contributed to the affordability of the design for many.

These aspects can be very well translated in small experimental buildings like pavilions and even follies if one wants to teach students a more hands-on construction-based holistic design approach. These pavilions can explore new ways of construction techniques and challenge the common understandings of space making. Their small scale and limitations on the usual multilayered approach of architectural assembly can focus on a particular idea that synthesizes the various complexities into one precise project that is reductive in both its conceptual and material natures.

I have often in my own teaching employed the making of smaller-scale buildings in order to teach construction, assembly, and craft. The students, working in teams or as individuals, are forced to translate conceptual ideas into built realities. In most cases, they lack the sophistication of the long history of building and craft intelligence that preceded centuries of refinement. Often connections are made with materials found in the local building supply shops based on household situations, like using a small steel angle with prearranged screw-holes to connect vertical to horizontal members. Invariably, this approach falters and produces wobbly and unsophisticated results. Techniques of woodworking, both in furniture making and building construction, can show how in previous decades, without 3D printing, continuous forces can be transferred by melting different components into one organism that maintains stability and coherence. These lessons are very important to architectural education since they teach conceptual clarity, material frugality, and constructive intelligence. When one can combine this activity with a social and cultural cause, in terms of its use and function, and if these objects can have an afterlife beyond their academic environment, then this exercise was a successful combination of teaching and acting in the world.

The projects undertaken in this book are sophisticated examples of students' engagement and constructive adventurism, aimed to add visual amusement and functional differentiation to sometimes neglected urban environments.

Mark Mack
Professor Emeritus, UCLA

[1] The MAK Center for Art and Architecture was created as a contemporary, experimental, multidisciplinary center for art and architecture headquartered in three significant architectural works by architect Rudolph Michael Schindler. It is supported by and affiliated with the MAK Vienna and administers a six-month residency program to aspiring artists.

Introduction

Architects oversee the entire process of buildings from their inception to their completion while collaborating with clients, engineers, builders, and local authorities to coordinate functional, aesthetic, practical, budgetary, structural, and legal matters on a given project. The role of contemporary architects no longer remains at an ordinary level (for example, designing and constructing beautiful, efficient, and safe buildings). Recently, the architect's role has expanded its responsibility beyond the realm of the traditional profession and from individual clients to public realms. While keeping their impact on society in mind, many architects pay attention to pro bono projects. Rather than designing and planning physical buildings, architects increasingly involve public services, recognizing the community's day-to-day life and creating excellent public buildings and places. A newfound priority for architects is to engage in creative collaborations with community members in the design of public realms by making structures, rejuvenating places, and working in different ways with local communities. Their involvement in local communities is an alternative type of pro bono practice toward sustainable, social, and humanitarian service in making a place or a community healthier, safer, and more livable.

The premise is a conspicuous phenomenon in the contemporary architectural profession. For shaping a better environment, architects volunteer or collaborate design tasks, legal matters, or first-hand construction experience in partnership with universities, local authorities, or diverse charitable organizations. Variable stakeholders engage with different community projects. Over the past few years, contemporary architects have played a proactive role in the social participation movement through talent donation and technical and legal assistance in collaboration with non-profit corporations, universities, and local authorities. Unlike typical architects, who work for specific clients, contemporary architects work for publicity. Their charitable acts reflect the zeitgeist of our time that values architects' pro bono service.

Why pavilions?

Pavilions in architecture typically refer to either subsidiary structures within the properties of an existing building site or building complex or independent structures within the space of an urban fabric. They are relatively smaller and lighter than building structures. Pavilions have striking relevance to the progress and status of the present society because pavilions tend to be the subject of contemporary architectural, conceptual, social, materialistic, technological, and structural issues. Accordingly, pavilion designs bring opportunities for innovative and radical concepts to be explored, tested, and experimented.

Public spaces do not necessarily look homogeneous or uniform. In recent times, architects have used pavilions as place makers to experiment with and showcase different design ideas, shedding light on critical issues of public concern. At times, they act as a marquee for special events. Pavilions also help shape public spaces, evoking curiosity and providing new inspiration for the people around. Although they reflect social, regional, and cultural connotations, some pavilion designs are entirely foreign in context or disassociated from their surroundings. The designs may have served as a testing ground for groundbreaking solutions, tools, instruments, and materials by implementing the latest tendencies in architecture. For that reason, pavilions vary from provocative ideas to social issues placed in any locations either at the heart of communities or in secluded spots. In some senses, they are valuable for architects to explore new creative ideas, opening new opportunities for architecture. The process of designing such pavilions is like that of discovery. They have a meaningful influence on creativity in architectural design discourse, research, and practice.

Although formally different, the pavilion is neither designated for a specific program nor bound to accommodate a series of functional usages. Perhaps, some pavilions serve specific purposes, such as hosting public events;

yet they are mainly open to the public or operated by users' desire to offer an opportunity for public occupation. For that reason, it can also be the space for unexpected activities that have not been planned. In several respects, pavilions serve as a central place to accommodate such unforeseen activities. Accordingly, at times, a large gap exists between the architect's intention of the design and the usage of the pavilion.

Neighborhoods within a community are places where communal activities occur. They include everyday places we meet and share, including kindergartens, streets, squares, parks, schools, and even marginal public areas. Pavilions in the community have become favorable. They allow community residents to become more connected. When located in public spaces, pavilions can promote social interaction and community association. Even if not grandiose, they can positively affect public areas in society and the surrounding environment. Small contributions may leverage big results. Architects' alternative roles are spotlighted to reshape small parcels of land or places within the neighborhood that we share.

Memory: a sense of place

Pavilions anchored in their open environment are interwoven with landscapes or cityscapes. A pavilion serves as a marquee that can gather people from surrounding areas. Each pavilion is centered on people and characterized depending on how they use or experience the place. Thus, the pavilion is the focal point of outdoor activity, whether playing, learning, resting, or others. The architecture, with its mix of meeting and event spaces, makes the pavilion a truly interactive place that enhances the quality of life of individuals in a neighborhood. In this case, pavilions are increasingly seen as community assets that offer various social, recreational, and cultural opportunities. A novel pavilion in an area has the potential to become an iconic landmark.

Unlike other types of pavilions that have specific purposes, community pavilions are defined by their unique relationships with individuals within the community. People spend time in pavilions to share stories about their daily lives, or to play and celebrate certain moments. The pavilion could become a part of the community's everyday life for many years and ultimately become a place where people's memories are accumulated. What is designed as a place for reset and recreation can then be transformed into a shelter for friendship and sharing of emotions such as joy, fear, anger, sadness, and love. Thus, the pavilion is not only a physical space but also a public one where social and psychological interactions happen.

Perhaps memory and place are strongly associated with the concerns of local identity emerging over the lifespan of pavilions.[1&2] People experience different elements of the physical environment, such as design, structure, and atmosphere, which combine to create a sense of place, and interpret them in their own way. Combined with their environment, people affect certain feelings and create an atmosphere. In particular, the unique design of the place contributes toward fashioning an individual or collective memory to legitimize local and cultural identities in certain places at particular times. The collective memory of the pavilion along with the surrounding area has a symbolic value.[3]

People accumulate memories of salient personal and public events and often recall a specific memory situated in time and space. With the passage of time, the memory remains a distinct sense of personal experience and place.[4] The pavilion serves as a multipurpose venue for events or a gathering place for social exchange. It also provides a recollection of past events with a spatial and temporal context. All of these constitute the construction of memory and nostalgia.

The place may play a crucial role in retrieving memory in a way that recalls the past. People trace their experiences and memories when they visit certain places. Events, activities, or theatrical presentations in the pavilion remain embedded in individual and collective memories. They are preserved in the public space and formed as public memory, which is constantly reassessed and revised through continual conversations in the public space. The temporal public memory always reoccurs in the same place. When revisited later, the place with the structure evokes many memories.

Thus, in designing a pavilion, the architect's compelling role, on the one hand, is to experiment with different materials, textures, structures, and spatial effects by testing new innovative forms, and on the other hand, to imagine the in situ relationship between memory and place through innovative engagement because architects take inspiration from site visits to develop their designs. In addition, some of the pavilions studied in this book are left unfinished without landscaping because the community's intervention has changed them, and the surrounding areas have grown physically through time. Furthermore, the structure has aged so the community gets together to repaint, repair, and maintain it by themselves. Because local residents have witnessed the process of the construction, operation, deterioration, and repair of community pavilions, they cherish the structure and place, and, of course, the memories made there.

Temporary structures and ephemeral ideas

Pavilions, by nature, are open-air temporary structures for specific events as well as neighborhood structures for daily activities. It is not only site-specific but also event specific. Pavilions host several activities and events and so their design is flexible, temporal, and open. Events play a significant role in nurturing and celebrating the culture and identity of a community or a city.

As pavilions provide the setting for community activities and events, they become permanent additions to the cityscape and allow public engagement with the surrounding context, thereby fostering a sense of place. Pavilions also accommodate intimate performances and activities according to the different qualities of the moment. They leave a mark of permanence on the places they engage with in the form of the memories they create, building upon unending layers of collective memory, emotion, and social relations. It is nested into a part of the community so that it provides a structure that triggers multiple uses and accommodates day-to-day activities for the neighbors. Such a public structure and place can become an essential element of a vibrant community. If designed well and completely integrated into the neighborhood, the pavilion will have a unique presence that can be passed on to future generations, giving the pavilion a timeless appeal. The development of pavilions does not have to conform to any typology or definition, nor does it have to refer to historical precedents. The universality of pavilion design implies that architects can consider designing one anywhere at any time.

Each pavilion design has a strong formal presence enhanced by its functional flexibility, which means that the functions of pavilions can be changed according to the users' needs and preferences. Thus, people who use pavilions can enjoy the versatility of the layout and the use of open space. Unlike typical architecture, pavilions are not structures where people live or work. Rather, pavilions are for resting, conversation, and quiet contemplation. Although pavilions are mostly small in our designs, they create a sense of place and pull people together. Their creative contribution becomes the basis of improving the urban atmosphere. In this case, pavilions have recently emerged as a kind of experimental building type that epitomizes the connection between building and place.

Although the physical structure has a short lifespan, the design concepts for pavilions last a long time. Thus, essential parts of the pavilion design do not necessarily mean durable materials and heavy structures on-site, but the memory of events or activities that the users have participated in. Of course, building a tangible object out of an architectural concept is significant, but the idea behind the design is also valuable.[5] At times, a unique building type represents the collective mindset of contemporary designers within the zeitgeist, and insightful reflection leads to certain designs. Pavilions can be fashioned to challenge routines and even to harmonize with the norms and trends of contemporary architecture. The design of pavilions may reflect the changing trends in architecture. The zeitgeist, in this sense, is the active engagement of the contemporary thoughts and ideas with the materials and structures of architecture.

Marginal practices

Pavilion design sometimes belongs to architecturally marginal practices. In recent years, the architectural profession has dramatically shifted its focus to experimental structures and the radical exploration of new designs with new material testing and developing new types of architectural designs.[6] The once-marginal practice has gradually found its way into an alternative approach to mainstream architectural discourse and is moving towards the center.

In addition, the latest trends show that many talented architects have participated in pavilion designs that serve as a testing ground for new ideas, materials, structural innovations, and design methods to unleash their design capabilities. Marginal does not mean insignificant. In contemporary society, pavilions have played a key role in the social functions of communities. At times, the pavilion becomes a social attraction because of its innovative design that creative architects have built in abandoned spaces.

The act of building pavilions aimed at public benefit has been subject to steady change over time, albeit with primarily locating in open public areas in recent years. Accordingly, pavilions have shifted their role to making the public space more inclusive, countering the use of privately owned public spaces in the past with inspiring designs. Many contemporary pavilions have attempted to explore how neglected places in various parts of a city might be retrieved or reclaimed as a shared public place to promote communal living. It may also contribute to an increase in the social and cultural value of the region.

The role of pavilion design is to intervene in existing context and social situations. Most projects in this book are treated as intermediate structures yet creative alternatives in the intersection of architecture and open scape. The structure has a physical presence that is partly open to the landscape and the architecture. It is neither interior nor exterior space, but a combination of both. Thus, the structure exists in a fuzzy territory of the built environment. The characteristics that define the architecture include openness, flexibility, ambiguity, and formlessness. The pavilion also has a characteristic that allows the user of the space to freely move through it.

A pavilion is not as concrete as a building. People do not typically inhabit pavilions but instead use them as a sheltered yet outdoor space where they can relax or spend some time. A retractable curtain or a camouflaged envelop may confuse the division between the interior and exterior spaces. Concerns about pavilion projects have shifted from form-making of freestanding structures to creating architectural environments, reconciling the architecture with open spaces. The pavilion typically blends with the natural or open scape and the structural forms may sometimes reflect the surrounding topography or merge entirely with the open scape. Thus, the external space traverses the structure and interlocks the interior and exterior.

Once seen as a marginal part of professional design practices, pavilions are now in the mainstream and have influenced contemporary design practices. However, the forms, styles, types, methods, and protocols involving pavilions still have a wide range of possibilities. A growing number of architects would like to participate and propose different ideas for pavilion designs. Numerous organizations and expositions have hosted various types of pavilion designs, thereby providing opportunities to test and exhibit new materials, spatial effects, forms, and designs. Perhaps a series of serpentine pavilions are good examples of spaces where architects can present their ideas every year.

Experimental showcase

Different pavilions may be found across a city, but most of them look mediocre. Today, the pavilion in a city landscape is increasingly significant and becoming a recognizable niche market within professional practice in architecture. The emergence of this niche market has been characterized not only by the use of new materials and technologies but also through greater levels of contribution by creative architects.

Although architects occasionally get involved in pavilion design, such projects are mainly motivated by commercial gains so the creative input into the pavilion design is insufficient. Not many manufacturers can develop original designs and they are mostly interested in keeping costs down when they work in niche markets. Accordingly, those who had been involved in most pavilion designs are not architects but manufacturers and business leaders who would oversee the design and manufacturing and control the costs. Most pavilions are either mass-produced and distributed by manufacturers or developed without architects so that the designs are substandard. Thus, the industry is regarded as a manufacturer's business rather than an architectural operation. These conditions must be resolved as the industry grows.

Inventive architects are increasingly involved in small pavilion projects that are considered experimental. Diverse types and purposes of pavilions in various scales have been designed throughout the world for expositions, events, fairs, resting tents, and street furniture. There is no limit to how pavilion design should be. It takes on all forms and functions from marquees to exhibition structures for expositions. Its open nature allows adequate scope to support forward-thinking design exploration. Therefore, pavilion designs literally extend the potential of architectural structures to new realms of creativity.

The pavilion becomes part of a manifesto from the critical point of view in architecture.

Nevertheless, it is futile to simply pursue new designs based on new materials and structures because a techno-oriented design is typically less creative. The once-marginal activity of architects has become a showcase and battleground for idea contests, which provide an opportunity to propose novel ideas without restrictions on creativity.

Not all pavilion designs are necessarily experimental in terms of new materials and techniques, but each architect aims to come up with their own concepts in an innovative manner. Exploration of creative designs from conventional materials and techniques is a challenging task. The designs could be considered by the architects as a way to explore and invent a new method that they have never adopted in their previous practices. Even if conventional materials are used, the designs may result in differences because of the architect's creativity.

As pavilions are comparatively small projects at a relatively low cost, young architects can use them as platforms to implement their architectural ideas. Accordingly, many young architects participate in creative pavilion designs that provide a platform to experiment with new ideas in the public realm. Thus, the pavilion becomes an indication of contributory forces and also serves as a gateway to creative design experiments that enable architects to make a name for themselves. The designs sometimes prove to be a creative endeavor that expresses the unique character of the architects.

Common materials yet uncommon designs

Pavilion design is classified as neither dogmatic style nor specific typology. There is neither a spatial diagram nor a form of convention for its spatial construction, unlike typical building designs.[7] The design character of a pavilion is open, flexible, and non-standardized, which means that the pavilion can be placed anywhere. By nature, pavilions are relatively simple and fast to construct and do not come with any limitations to their use.

Serpentine Gallery Pavilion, Selgas Cano, 2015

Student Pavilion Design, University of Hawaii at Manoa, 2001

Pavilion design allows architects to cultivate new ideas and create an excellent platform to experiment with new architectural types. However, the "material must always be subservient to the idea and should never direct it," as Semper asserted.[8] The pavilions also become an opportunity to implement new materials and construction technologies. Their novel forms and eye-catching designs not only attract the attention of spectators but also stimulate the emergence of new styles.[9]

Various design ideas with the materials provide infinite aesthetic possibilities capable of surpassing traditional stylistic canons to create the hallmarks of surrounding areas. For a series of pavilions in the book, engineering lumber was repeatedly used as a motif along with exterior layers of exposed lumber. The choice of the material was not the deciding factor in the embodiment of the designs. However, to a great extent, engineering lumber is the most basic and easy-to-handle material available and it is also reliable for the use of pavilion design and construction. The process of cutting and assembling the timbers is also straightforward. Timbers were chosen with consideration of colors and textures because they are perfect materials to use in a particular landscape and cityscape.

From one perspective, the timber structure may look common or perhaps mediocre. However, engineering timber does not have limitations in creative design. Even if they look commonplace, the materials present a dynamic image that grows and changes, creating a sculptural form according to the designs of architects. The fixed standardized timber becomes the perfect material for flexible pavilion design. As Loos asserted, "every material possesses its own language of forms"[10] to help shape the design and construction of pavilion forms. And as Schindler wrote, "certain form is asking for definite material,"[11] and "certain material is asking for definite form." Conventional materials do not have design restrictions even in contemporary forms. Innovation in the design and manufacturing process enables architects to recreate authentic details. The original design can be achieved by integrating conventional materials while creatively reassembling them.

In a series of projects in the book, the horizontally and vertically aligned lumbers with the members stand out from the distance. They are bolted to the base and connected to the foundation. A juxtaposition of the unit lumbers creates a rhythm. Different sizes of industrial lumbers, such as 2 by 2 inches, 2 by 4 inches, 4 by 4 inches, and 2 by 6 inches, form different dimensions of linear repetition.

The ways industrial lumbers are repeatedly lined up display serial patterns produced by a single individual component or alternatingly arrayed by using different components. Each component is set without a hierarchical order.[12] The components control the interval between lines in the structure. Each piece of lumber as a modular element is stretched out at certain intervals. Seen in combination with the use of industrial materials and techniques, the repeated compositions of the lumber highlight the identity at a distance from the aesthetic goals away from the surroundings.

Repetition is a core method used in designing a series of pavilions in this book and reflects the basic uniformity of the pavilion. The layout of serial lumbers stimulates a rhythmic texture or creates an abstract pattern that provides unique styles. The design resembles an open framework where explicit vertical and horizontal lines are repeatedly aligned. Despite its clarity in form and transparency in structure, the repetition yields a subtle illusion. Part of the illusion is due to repeating the placement of lumbers at regular intervals. The serial repetition of the component establishes a heightened spatiotemporal intimacy between the structure and the viewer. In addition, even if the structure is totally blocked with a wall, it provides a silhouette against the other side of the room. A series of rhythms of the same type is repeatedly formed on the floor and wall so that the pavilion structure shares an identical style. Repeating the materials in vertical and horizontal strips at regular intervals creates a radical homogeneity and redundancy of form very much like Carlo Scarpa's building details. Such a monotonic pattern is particularly evident in Sauerbruch Hutton's recent building, the Brandhorst Museum in Munich (2008–11), which is clad with strips of colored ceramic louvers. The repeating patterns with colors are not banal but rather produce a repeated harmony that awakens joy in the observer.[13]

Such serial approaches have been extensively adopted by abstract minimalist artists as a means to present their artwork. The redundant patterns and rows of the geometric configuration are reminiscent of the serial arts tradition that flourished into various abstract painters' drawings. The parallels between such compositions and the works of Frank Stella, Josef Albers, Sol LeWitt, Bridget Riley, Max Bill, Morris Louis, Kenneth Noland, and Andrzej Nowacki are striking. The patterns are common to minimal abstract art and are the result of using the properties of industrially produced materials.

From conventional to idiosyncratic

Designing an idiosyncratic pavilion is a different approach from designing a conventional one. For inventive architects, creativity is an essential part of their unique work, which requires steady effort and patience to turn ideas into viable results. A large amount of trial and error is also necessary before certain ideas come to fruition. Very few designs are a showcase of novel ideas and creative solutions that lead to a new aesthetic trend. While many of the pavilions today remain ordinary in terms of style, structure, details, and typologies, many others are the outcomes of outlandish proposals.

A compelling vision and a fresh way of looking at design issues is essential for a creative individual to come up with a revolutionary design. Paradigm changes in architecture often happen when new design methods or approaches are introduced, which radically alter the conceptual or manufacturing process of a design. The paradigm shift lies at the core of the architectural profession and, of course, inspires visionary ideas for the future. However, some conceptual designs are hardly followed by construction. They remain in a design laboratory or exist only on paper.

Architects are willing to take part in a creative activity that gives them an opportunity to experiment with new ideas. Pavilions have been a good testing ground for innovative design solutions. A fine-tuned experimental design has been a positive influence on creativity in architectural discourse. Architects can shape the emergence of a compelling idea and a well-articulated vision that resonates with countless people, inspires them to learn more, and compels them to shift their perspectives. The goal of these architects is to think outside the normal box. Visionary thinking as a creative act could be a key to achieving new tendencies in architecture. It enables architects to imagine new possibilities. Accordingly, many designs could become visionary projects.

Developing ideas, implementing visions in groundbreaking designs, and constructing novel structures that are reliable and impressive remain a challenge. Owing to new possibilities in design, pavilions also involve atypical and unconventional construction processes. The workflow is also significantly different to that of conventional buildings. At times, all components are different in shape and detail, so a highly integrative process is essential to ensure effective construction. Each component of the pavilion is precisely prefabricated and delivered to the job site for assembly, and then the kit-of-parts construction becomes easy to perform on any site. Without any loss of precision, the construction workflow allows for addressing design, structure, and construction considerations concurrently. Typically, construction takes an incredibly short time from commissioning to opening, but the entire workflow requires careful design and detailing. Assembly from the scale of the overall structure down to the minute details needs to be explored through a continuous improvement feedback process to implement the structure with little hassle. The precisely simulated workflow serves as a platform to investigate the processes during manual assembly in greater detail.

Designing a pioneering pavilion is a new opportunity to explore or discover new ideas. The newly unveiled innovative designs mostly require new ways of manufacturing. In this study, research and experimentation in different ways, perhaps beyond the boundaries of the profession, are needed to find the best way to develop the design or create something new. These designs require the

The Cloud, Department of Architecture, Inha University, 2015

use of various materials and skill sets. Thus, finding new ways of production is necessary to fulfill specific tasks with the most desirable skill sets different from those applied in the current building industry. A radically new approach is needed in both design and production.

Social entrepreneurship

Pavilion designs on a small parcel of a derelict area or unused land, perhaps on the edge of a community, can be transformed into a vibrant public space. The transformation of these areas into communal spaces is essential to urban renewal, resilience, and vigor. However, it is not possible to reuse all empty urban spaces as community spaces. Caution must be taken to find a potential area for alternative public reuse. We are aware of how the dynamic value of the areas and pavilion designs become a powerful instrument of transformation.

The pro bono participation of various stakeholders plays a significant role in the success of such projects. Participating professional architects also play a pivotal role in implementing and successfully constructing designs on the jobsite. Due to the course of funding, planning, designing, and constructing, strategies and procedures are needed to reuse derelict areas to recreate communal spaces. Despite the noble concept of rejuvenating an area by creating a pavilion, various strategies and procedures in execution should be contrived because different groups of participants must be engaged. The entire process is a collaborative act. In the following, we define the notion and procedures involved in building pavilions for giving.

Derelict areas: not a hot potato but an opportunity

Derelict areas are ubiquitous in a community, but they negatively impact neighborhoods, attracting crime and anti-social behavior, illegal dumping of waste, committing vandalism, becoming overgrown, or being frowned upon. Many areas in a community remain as such for a long time and face pressures for sustainable regeneration and spatial renewal of areas.[14&15] Such places must be reshaped and recovered for everyday activities. If one observes a surrounding community, one will find a kit of marginal areas that are unused, deteriorated, or abandoned. More hollow spaces are anticipated because of the rapid expansion and aging of cities. Regenerating such spaces plays a critical part in contemporary architecture because they serve to improve the local environment and reshape the community's image.

In this respect, turning derelict areas into community assets is the primary focus of the design research by providing an opportunity to reinterpret the abandoned areas and proposing new design options. This approach will contribute to the act of placemaking, in which communities use areas that are identified by a collective cultural space. Essentially, the strategy is closely connected to make better buildings, places, communities, and cities.

Unfortunately, derelict areas are often located in poorer, more deprived areas and are highly likely to demonstrate the aging phenomenon of a city. Bringing abandoned urban places back into productive use for a community could help create more resilient communities. Derelict areas mean large-scale lots and small-scale, run-down, and negligent areas that can be found anywhere around a community. They include gaps in between buildings, or spaces such as verges, and are adjacent to buildings. Much of the derelict lands have been largely ignored, but these could be transformed into playgrounds, shelters, and areas for greenery and flora to be planted. For years, they have been waiting to be adapted to the existing urban fabric or reutilized as part of attractive urban spots.

Transforming derelict areas into community activity areas can be significant in improving the community environment and life. With the collaboration of community members, areas could be converted into community pavilions and pocket parks for the elderly, playgrounds for the youth, and resting shelters for residents. The areas will hold outdoor community activities and places for social gatherings to enhance community wellbeing. Initiatives that involve people in reclaiming lands more productively can create a real sense of neighborhood belonging. By working together with various stakeholders, people in neighborhoods can feel more empowered and connected to their local area.

For architects, the areas should not be considered a risk factor for urban decline but rather a window of opportunity for a better community. If well planned and designed, pavilions could have a lasting effect on an abandoned site, thus making the derelict areas equitable, sustainable, and accessible to the local community. Derelict areas in public realms have been transformed with the primary target of repurposing by adding new designs, creating stunning spaces, and integrating into a community.

Praxis and pro bono activity

Professional architects are used to designing buildings for clients within professional ethics, standards, and applicable legal requirements. They typically strive to find better design choices or alternative design solutions that meet most clients' requirements within a reasonable time and that utilize available budgets and resources. Given that architects primarily work for clients who pay for their fees, much of their activities occur when they obtain economic benefits from their professional work. Given that their engagements are limited to economic gains and benefits of their services, their exposure to the public is limited. While ordinary architects are faithful to architectural services, limiting themselves to mediocre and mundane works, creative architects may not pursue normal or cliché designs. These architects spend a considerable amount of time and effort exploring new ideas and concepts by utilizing different techniques and design representations.

Likewise, architects who value creative designs will seriously work on every step of their designs. These architects are supposed to be equipped with theoretical and practical knowledge that can be enacted, practiced, embodied, or realized throughout professional practices. Theory and practice are not separate entities, yet both have a dialectical relation that helps each other. For such architects, praxis would have been referred to as the notion beyond the productive activity for constructing a building. Architects tend to be innovative, creative, and often playful to meet the demands of building new outputs and services successfully. Theory in connection to design practice plays a crucial role in the generation of creative architecture. Equipped with theory, critical ideas, and beliefs, such creative architects always search for new, original, and inspirational ideas. Theoretical knowledge does not mean technical aids necessary to produce architectural output, but it helps architects stimulate creative and inspirational thinking in accomplishing their design practices.

With praxis in mind, the social role of architects has become increasingly emphasized for the contemporary architectural society to engage more professional architects in everyday practical action that affects the daily life of human beings. The architect's social contribution reflects the spirit of the times. Patterns of professional architecture practice have gradually weighed on architects' social roles and contributions to the society they belong to, much beyond the scope of their conventional works. The gradual paradigm shift affects architectural practices toward living together. This shift in professional attitude demands architects' social role and anthropophilic behavior suitable for the new era. The traditional notion of praxis should be sophistically incorporated with a robust action toward helping and supporting a better community. Perhaps, the pro bono practice is the most significant responsibility of architects to the public. Besides offering professional legal, social, and design services for societal projects without fees, architects provide their time, talent, and voluntary labor to achieve social impact for a range of community groups. Lately, architects' pro bono practice has been a growing interest within the profession.

Through these activities, architects use their design skills, experiences, and knowledge to benefit communities. Their activities involve voluntary design, consulting, and legal services with no compensation. Architects will gain rewards from the activities in other ways, including better connection to the community, good publicity, and social and clientele relations. However, that will not be their ultimate goal. Their goals contain deeply rooted thoughts on the good effects and attitudes of architecture on society. They are based on their social contribution to humanitarian aspects. That is, architecture serves society to improve the quality of life and the environment. More noble architects would engage in the opportunity within their professional roles to make and sustain a better environment for a community through association with the charity that includes voluntary activities.

Platform: a base for community partnership

Several participants would have been involved in each pro bono project from private and public sectors, including universities, local businesses, non-profits, communities, and local government offices. Empowering the effective partnership among these groups is fundamental for the success of each project. The partnership influences a positive effect that opens possibilities of new collaboration among different groups and builds a better community ideal for residents. To fulfill effective partnerships, proactive leadership is paramount. Within the existing Design Research and Innovation Laboratory (D-Lab) in the Department of Architecture at Inha University, Korea, a new type of platform was launched to heighten the collective efforts of different partnerships. It will serve as a vehicle used for pro bono activity. The lab will be a place where researchers, professionals, donors, local government authorities, and community neighbors meet to develop more thriving and inspiring designs for the community.

Given the nature of each project, many different sectors must be brought into play to strengthen the capacity for professional and institutional development, having platforms that gather people from different professions and backgrounds, manage and facilitate initiatives, and coordinate all stakeholders.

D-Lab brings forth innovative design ideas and solutions by connecting hands-on designs and details with research for a specific site. Each project begins with a meeting within the community to advocate the project. It achieves different levels of community engagement, from consultation to co-creation. Partnerships need to work with local government authorities to cultivate projects while simultaneously conducting design research on each project to meet the community's needs. D-Lab has worked closely with community groups to enable dialogue, establish partnerships with the community, and articulate what pavilions the communities need. Given that obtaining funding from an outside source is indispensable for implementing each project, the partnership should apply for support grants or arrange for various meetings to raise funds. At times, the lab draft proposals that cogently describe the importance of the coalition's mission, articulate why it is legitimate and representative of the community, and specify how the requested funding will enable the coalition to accomplish its mission-related goals.

Similar to clients approaching architects for projects, the platform is operated to find issues, sites, and problems in a community and then proposes potential changes and ideas to activists in the community and local government authorities to improve the site. At times, citizens are approached to ask for advice. Researchers from the lab develop innovative ideas and solutions to the challenges being faced or at times requested by the public. In the meantime, the lab searches for donors, including social donation organizations and businesses.

Architecture students' voluntary involvement is also significant in the success of each project. However, academic initiatives that support social contribution are still lacking. In this respect, architectural education has been lagging. Clinging to traditional teaching methods and old-fashioned curriculum, architectural programs offer outdated content that may not be up to current or future requirements.

Lately, more architecture schools have been involved in community initiative programs in the studio setting. Students under the direction of faculty members experience and learn more about the architectural profession by participating in public services. Public-engaged learning offers valuable benefits for all participating students. Perhaps, one of the most significant benefits of the approach has been the production of the pavilion at low budgets.

First-hand participation for sweat equity

Architects typically work a lot of hours. They spend most of their time at an office desk, where they develop ideas, draw plans, meet with clients, and consult with engineers, but they still visit jobsites to oversee the construction and review the progress of projects. In contemporary practice, individual contractors, not architects, must be intimately familiar with every nut and bolt of construction as the work progresses. Although architects, consultants, and contractors collaborate intensively to work out the nuts and bolts of the building and develop the required documentation, architects are rarely involved in a sweat equity project such as those outlined in this book.

The sweat equity approach to the pavilion projects is described as a unique process for participating stakeholders in severely deteriorated neighborhoods. Within the sweat equity framework, each participant contributes a specified amount of voluntary labor during the design and construction phase.

The projects that appear in this book take the theme "pavilions for giving," where each project is set to be a bold showcase of experimental yet unique pavilion designs for the chosen site. Part of the benefit of participating in a series of projects is doing some design exercise and building the design. Being part of the projects from inception to construction is a rare opportunity for students and architects.

The projects share the underlying common thread. Conventional timber material marries innovative design ideas that accentuate the pavilion's unique necessities and places. Each pavilion design responds to requests by end-users for their everyday activity in a community and specific site. In the design phase of the project, one or more designs are developed, exploring the site, and proposing structural and assembly details of the project. Laboratory researchers explore various design ideas to gain and brainstorm insights into the pavilion design and experiment with some practical techniques to help achieve the final design. Researchers produced several mock-up models by performing details, joints, and structural strength. The final design is showcased through diverse mock-up models with detailed study models and presented to end-users to gather feedback.

Once a project is determined to proceed after a series of discussions and citizens, donors, and local authorities are all satisfied with the design, D-Lab starts making plans, details, and documents to carry out the project. All necessary drawings, details, hardware, assembly tools, and fabrication plans are prepared. In the project's construction phase, the pavilion is fabricated on a real scale in the chosen site. All participants and professionals and, at times, donors take part in the construction process of the pavilions. Every participants' effort makes a difference across a range of manufacturing operations in the construction site. As such, the final built pavilion is the fruit of all participants' combined effort and hard work.

All voluntary participants dedicate their time and effort to ensure the success of each project. Sweat equity marks all participants' pro bono efforts. Witnessing the impact and change of the areas on the spot is a valuable experience. All agree that being a part of pro bono work offers the most rewarding experiences professionally and personally. Pavilions embody the hard work, sweat, and skills of participants, making them truly a team effort. The whole process establishes the community neighbors' equity venture.

Six interventions: creative alternatives

The pavilions in this book were built through a series of organized seminars, lectures, roundtable discussions, and workshops hosted by D-Lab. At times, speakers and architects were invited to give talks or to share their experience with the participants. Various strategies and design methods were fused and evolved in each of the projects with different skill sets. Some of the constructing techniques were accumulated and replicated for future pavilion projects. Every project involved different design and construction activities specific to each product, but the key idea behind each stage remained the same. Most of these pavilions were an opportunity for creating a place to be used by everyone and made by everyone.

Several projects have been carried out involving public and private collaboration in the name of social contribution and talent offering. D-Lab spearheaded most of the activities, including planning, designing, fundraising, finding donors, and even administrative tasks. The entire construction was conducted with the help of people who volunteered to participate. Each project was given to communities or public facilities after it was completed, and once participants had contributed their time, effort, and energy to each project.

Students have the chance to participate from project planning to completion and donation. Professional architects assisted the students in resolving technical issues and in securely constructing each piece in the series. Students' participation is a type of learning and gift of talent, similar to how professional architects carry out pro bono services. In a contemporary society, an architect's work entails much more than simply designing and constructing functional, efficient, pleasant, and attractive structures. It is a broad scope that extends beyond the traditional methods.

For example, participation in socially driven initiatives is also the architects' responsibility and may be the most effective contribution that helps in improving the environment and society. It is not only an act of giving money, goods, or something of monetary value to another person or organization at no cost but also an act of offering opportunities to aid communities in collaboration with universities, professional architects, and the local government.

We devoted special attention to deprived and derelict areas that have been stigmatized for a long time. Residents' dread of criminality intensifies because the areas are perceived as neglected and filthy. The number of abandoned areas in a neighborhood might be a good indicator of how underdeveloped or miserable it is. Finding a site for each project raises awareness of dark areas, built and unbuilt spaces, and urban neighborhoods that surround us, and fosters sensitivity toward the areas we live in.

The goal of each project is to provide new pavilions for socially vulnerable individuals of a community by renovating neglected areas. These spaces, which were previously abandoned, will be transformed into a positive place that will not only improve the local environment but also inspire residents' sense of community. Such areas will be used as a venue for socially marginalized classes to communicate, socialize, or participate in cultural engagement. A pavilion is provided on one side of an old and shabby alley for children to run about or for residents to rest and share their everyday lives across generational divides and ages.

The plan was to complete one project per year. Each project was uniquely developed, taking into consideration the site situation of the target areas, and reflecting the requests of recipients. It was created by architectural students and researchers in a studio setting through discussions and design development. After experimenting with various ideas, a design was chosen, and the materials, details, manufacturing, and assembly method were then tested.

Lumber is an environmentally friendly material that may be used in public facilities. Each pavilion proves to be a creative experience that offers a sense of geometric unity and rhythmic recurrence using simple dimensional lumbers. Distinctive designs were created by rhythmically repeating or shaping curvatures, arraying layers of surfaces, or expressing streamlined shapes. Different designs, details, and materials for each project were uniquely used in consideration of the attributes of the chosen sites and users.

Multiple mock-up models were developed to examine and identify the factors that could impact the structural stability and safety. Several design modifications were made to alleviate issues that occur during the manufacturing. Concerns, such as stability issues, work tools, materials, and construction methods, have become important determinants for each pavilion because the design and fabrication were carried out by students rather than professional contractors. Hence, professional assistance was required for structural and constructional issues in each project.

This book documents the entire design and the assembly process of each pavilion, including the underlying concept, design development, detailing, joinery, and construction. Each project was distinct and significant in contributing to the dilapidated areas in the neighborhoods, yet the overall process involves a long and stressful experience. Nonetheless, it was a great opportunity for students and architects who took part to experience the joy of sharing their time and talent.

Notes

1. Frances Yates, *The Art of Memory* (Harmondsworth, Middlesex: Penguin Books, 1978).
2. Christian Norberg-Schulz, *Genius Loci: Towards a Phenomenology of Architecture* (New York: Rizzoli, 1979).
3. Aldo Rossi, *The Architecture of the City* (Cambridge: The MIT Press, 1984).
4. Stark, Shauna M. and Craig E. L. Stark (eds.), "Introduction to memory," *Neurobiology of Language* (Cambridge: Academic Press, 2016), 841–845.
5. Jin-Ho Park, "The Underlying Geometry in Rudolph M. Schindler's Packard House," *Journal of Asian Architecture and Building Engineering*, vol. 12 (2013): 9–15.
6. Hensel, Michael and Christian Hermansen Cordua, "Past and Present Trajectories of Experimental Architectures," *Architectural Design*, vol. 85 (March 2015): 16–23.
7. Witold Rybczynski, *The Look of Architecture* (New York: Oxford University Press, 2001).
8. Wolfgang Herrmann, *Gottfried Semper: In Search of Architecture* (Cambridge: The MIT Press, 1989).
9. Shigeru Ban, *Shigeru Ban: Material, Structure and Space* (Tokyo: Toto Publishing, 2017).
10. Adolf Loos, *Spoken into the Void: Collected Essays 1897–1900* (Cambridge: The MIT Press, 1982).
11. Rudolph Michael Schindler, 1916, unpublished manuscript in archives at the Architectural Drawing Collection, The University Art Museum, University of California, Santa Barbara.
12. John Coplans, "Serial Imagery," *Artforum* (September 1968), 34–43.
13. Charles Jencks, "Architecture Becomes Music," *The Architectural Review* (May 2013), 91–108.
14. Cramer, Johannes and Stefan Breitling (eds), *Architecture in Existing Fabric: Planning, Design, Building* (Basel: Birkhäuser, 2007).
15. Charles Bloszies, *Old Buildings, New Designs* (New York: Princeton Architectural Press, 2012).

References

Djokic, Vladan, Ana Nikezic and Natasa Jankovic, "Socially Responsible Architect – Towards Creating Place." In Satish Narayanasamy (ed.), *International Conference on Social Science and Management* (ICSSM2014) (Lancaster: DEStech Publications, Inc., 2014): 169–176.

Gottfried Semper, *The Four Elements of Architecture and Other Writings* (Cambridge: Cambridge University Press, 1989).

Jin-Ho Park, *Architectural Experiments and Lessons Toward Innovative Designs* (Seoul: Spacetime, 2015).

Jin-Ho Park, *Graft in Architecture: Recreating Spaces* (Melbourne: Images Publishing, 2013).

Margaret Crawford, "Can Architecture Be Socially Responsible?" in Diane Ghirardo (ed), *Out of Site: A Social Criticism of Architecture* (Seattle: Bay Press, 1991): 27–45.

Palich, Natasha and Angelique Edmonds, "Socially Sustainability: Creating Places and Participatory Processes that Perform Well for People", *EDG78NP* (November 2013): 1–13.

Pearson, Jason and Mark Robbins (eds), *University-Community Design Partnerships: Innovation in Practice* (New York: Princeton Architectural Press, 2002).

Scott Bernhard, "Notes on the Intersection of Architecture and Social Entrepreneurship," *Fall Conference Proceedings*, ACSA (October 2014): 263–72.

Sharon Haar, "Architecture's New Social Entrepreneurial Networks," *REbuilding*, ACSA National Conference, New Orleans, Louisiana (March 2010): 580–587.

Sylvia Lavin, "Vanishing Point: The Contemporary Pavilion," *Artforum International*, vol.51 (October 2012): 212–219.

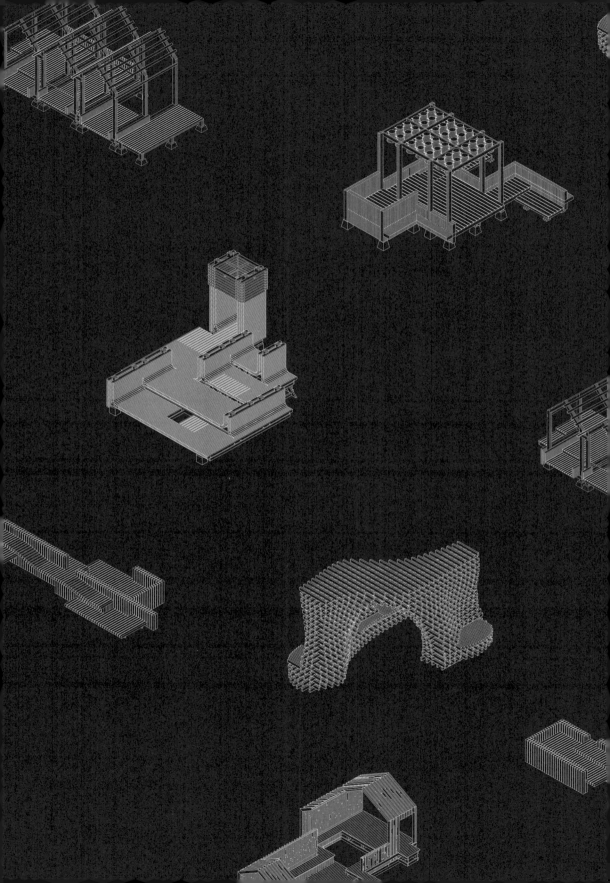

Six Works

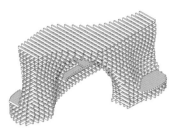

Street Pavilion

Vacant yard in front of the Embassy of Canada
Jeongdong, Seoul, Korea
2014

The Street Pavilion was built to commemorate the fiftieth anniversary of diplomatic relations between Korea and Canada through the collaboration of D-Lab and Canada Wood Korea. The funding was provided by Canada Wood Korea and the project was sponsored by the Embassy of Canada to Korea.

The pavilion was built in front of the embassy in Jeongdong, Seoul, in an open area surrounding a 500-year-old tree. Given that the open area is relatively large, the embassy wanted to install a pavilion for public use. Jeongdong has long been regarded as one of the most beautiful, genteel, romantic, historic, and cultural neighborhoods. The main street in Jeongdong goes along the stonewall walkway of Deoksu Palace and is lined with historical buildings. The pavilion was built close to an old tree in front of the embassy without obstructing pedestrian traffic.

While allowing the pedestrian-priority street to remain uncluttered, the pavilion provides an active front to the embassy building around the edges of the street. Locating seats at the pavilion provides users with an opportunity to watch passersby and look upon the surrounding area.

The project employed a strategy to connect the cross axes of the pedestrian traffic flow. One axis is located between the main entrance of the embassy and the old tree, and the other axis is the pre-existing sidewalk. We wanted to create a pavilion where people may pass by or rest for a while so we created two independent islands to accommodate the flow of pedestrians. Each island is located on either side of the sidewalk. The tops of the two islands were joined to form a single mass. Structural stability was established due to the weight of the upper structure. It allows pedestrians to walk through the pavilion and down the roadway at the same time. After the creation of a streamlined shape, it was dissected at regular intervals to match the size of the straight dimensional lumber. Although various methods for efficiently connecting lumbers were considered, we decided to cut grooves and weave the components together.

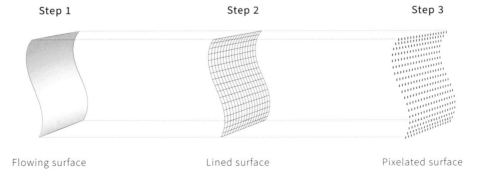

Step 1 — Flowing surface
Step 2 — Lined surface
Step 3 — Pixelated surface

Sidewalk

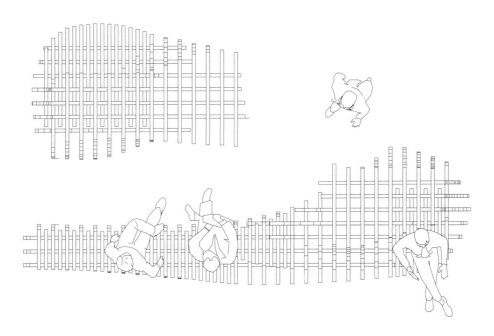

Embassy of Canada building

The pavilion is located in the middle of the sidewalk; hence, it is easily spotted while strolling during the daytime. At night, this structure could be a hindrance to traffic because of the dim streetlights. A glow-in-the-dark paint was added to the end face of each component to improve awareness of the night street traffic, allowing the pavilion to be easily recognized from a distance, while also serving as an important landmark in the night streets. The pavilion may be seen as a collection of luminous dots.

After the design was finalized, the grooves and methods of assembly underwent extensive scrutiny. The size, depth, and position of the connection joints and grooves of each component were accurately identified and precise drawings were produced. The 3D assembly process of the structure was verified using a computer program. All the components were tangled together and supported by the vertical loads because there is no foundation for the structure.

The pre-incised Douglas fir 2x4 lumber was used for the structure. The lumbers were woven into each other's grooves to ensure that each component of the upper and the lower parts was joined together and fastened with stainless steel screws for the structural stability and the integrity of the structure. If the grooves were considerably deep, this could compromise the structure's stability. Hence, we decided to cut less than 20 percent of the depth of the upper and lower parts of the component.

After the lumbers were delivered for cutting, we chose to exclude some with bends and knots to ensure the overall stability of the structure. Each set of components was fabricated off-site, cut, and grooved according to the sizes and locations of every component using the table saws. The assembly order was identified by marking each part with pen to ensure the correct sequence. Then, the overall assembly was simulated. Thirty students carried out the cutting and grooving of the components in a vacant lot on campus for approximately five days. An expert from Canada Wood Korea helped students safely cut and assemble all the pieces. All drawings of every component were printed and accurately cut with cutters according to its size, length, and length of the grooves. After cutting grooves with a trimmer tool, the finishing work was carried out by hand with a chisel.

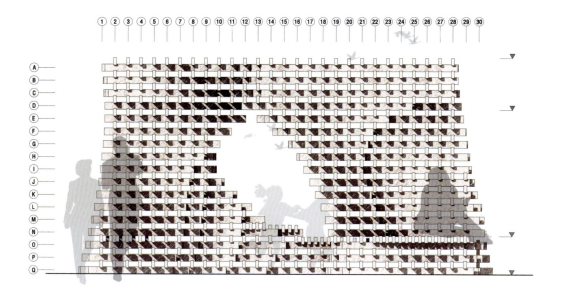

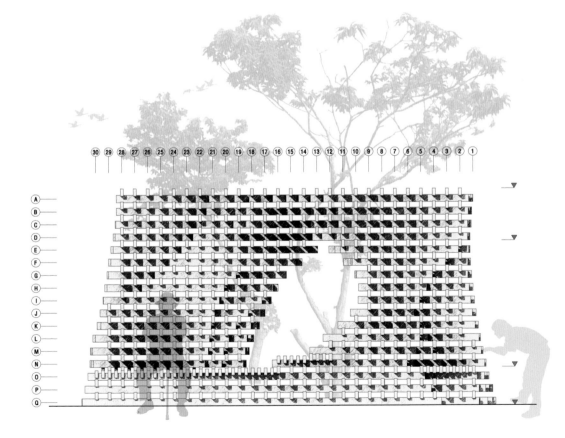

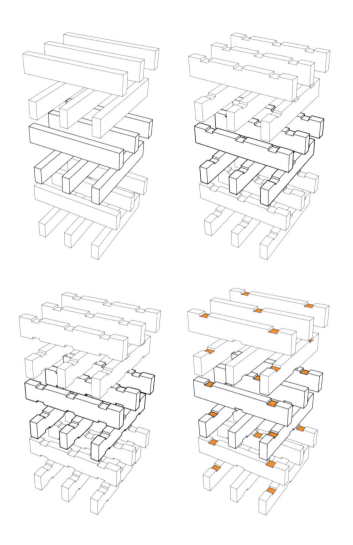

Grooves cut with hand chisels

Roof

The tops of the two islands are connected to a single mass. The weight of the roof structure above is transmitted to other structural elements below through compression.

Column

While checking the spacing and distance of each component accurately, the components are stacked, layer by layer.

Bottom

The components at the bottom are placed in the correct position without the structural foundation.

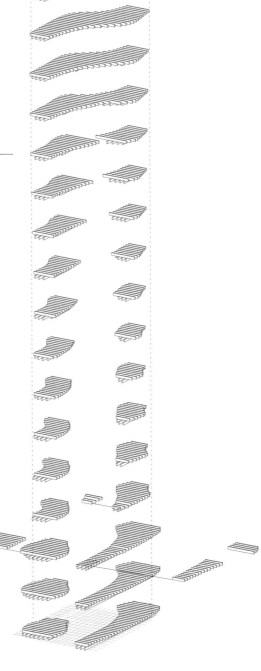

Structural assembly

The width, depth, height, and position of the grooves of each component are marked at the correct location. All the components are joined together using stainless steel L-shaped brackets and screws.

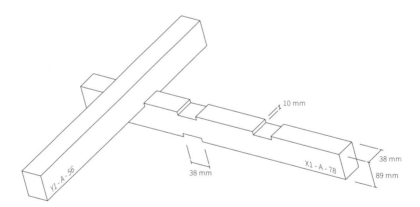

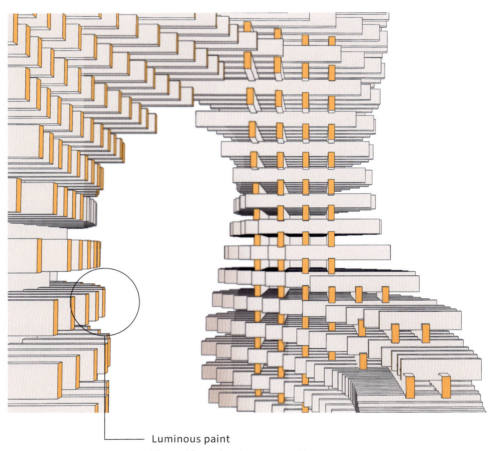

Luminous paint
The end face of each component is coated with glow-in-the-dark paint so that the pavilion can be easily recognized in the dark.

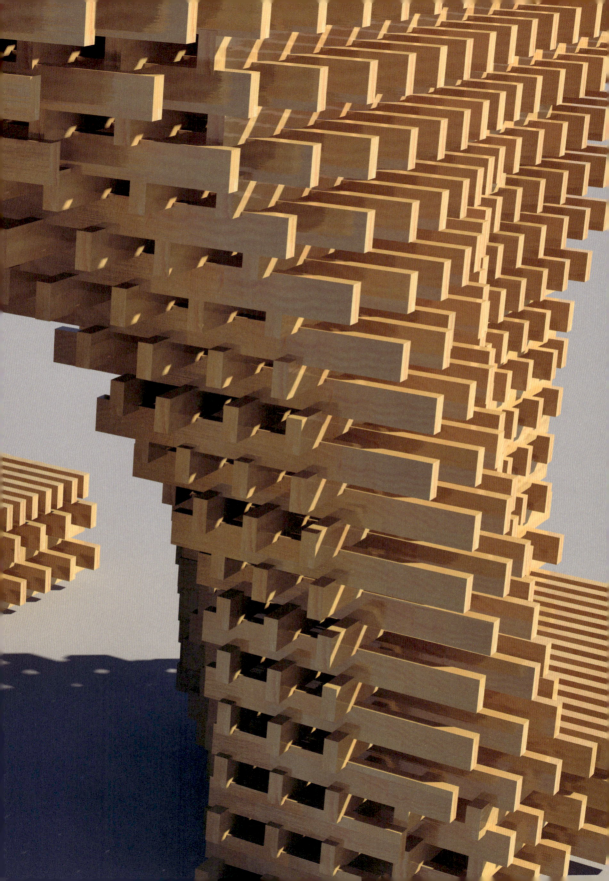

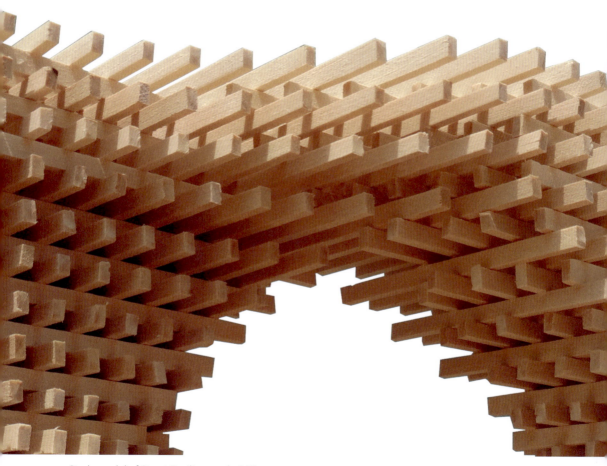
Study model of Street Pavilion, scale 1:20

Study model

Several scaled study models of the design were fabricated and then evaluations were performed on design elements, notches, joinery, finishes, and structural stability. Comparing study models helps the design team agree on a design direction. Once the study models are presented to stakeholders, a more detailed visual criticism is obtained on the spot. In addition, the realistic depictions make it simple to assess what makes sense about the designs from the user's perspective.

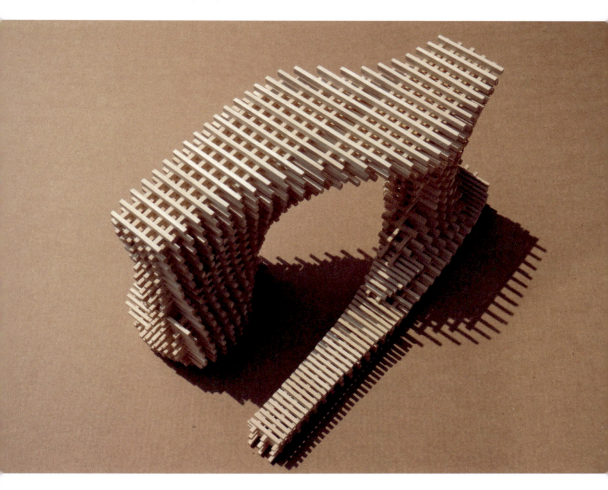

All components are coded and grouped before being factory-treated with alkaline copper quaternary (ACQ) preservative for two weeks.

Each component of the bottom part is laid out correctly and double-checked for accuracy. The components are woven into each other's grooves and then fastened with stainless steel screws.

Participants check the spacing and distance of the structure.

After all components were cut, these were grouped and transported to the factory for preservative treatment for two weeks. Alkaline copper quaternary (ACQ) preservative was applied. ACQ is a water-based wood preservative that prevents lumber from rotting by insects and fungi. This substance has been broadly used for timbers, decks, fence posts, and other wood structures because it is considered low risk in relation to its impact on human health and the environment. Finally, all components were organized as assembly kits and transported to the jobsite after antiseptic treatment. The components were classified and assembled in the predetermined order, and each connection part was fixed using stainless steel screws for the structural solidity. Luminous paint was applied on the structure facing a dark street and sidewalk. At night, the luminous paint glows, and pedestrians can easily recognize the pavilion from a distance, like a beacon.

The surrounding edges are wrapped with tape so they remain unpainted.

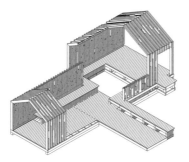

Courtyard Hideout

Shinmyeoung Daycare Center
749 Gyeongin-ro, Bupyeong-gu, Incheon, Korea
2015

For the Courtyard Hideout project, the lumbers were sponsored by local lumber vendor NSHome, and the expenses of renting tools and purchasing hardware were covered by a local branch of Christian Business Men's Connection (CBMC). An architect from TCM Global, Jaecheol Choi, helped NSHome donate lumbers for the project and then assisted the students to safely construct the pavilion.

The site is located in a small backyard between a church and a small staff accommodation at Shinmyeoung Daycare Center in Bupyeong-gu, Incheon. The center is a type of residential care that accommodates a large group of orphan children (children without parents) until they become independent at nineteen years old. The same services are provided to all children irrespective of their gender, age, needs, and reasons for separation from parents. The service provision is typically depersonalized, and strict routines are followed by a small number of staff. At times, children living in the center are isolated from the community because their situation means they are unable to maintain social and/or family relationships. This project intends to provide children with the opportunity to play and spend individual time outside.

The director of the center expressed a concern that the facility was not able to afford any exterior structure for children to rest and enjoy outdoor classes and activities. In keeping with the theme of the center, we proposed a pavilion design outdoors, where children can relax, play musical instruments, prepare small performances, and read books. The pavilion is situated on a 15-by-25-meter plot of land surrounded by pine and bamboo trees. The grassy area had remained untouched for a long time and seemed perfectly suited for the pavilion.

Step 1

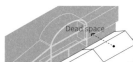

Initial massing

Step 2

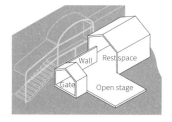

Assigning programs

Step 3

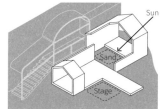

Carving partial designs out

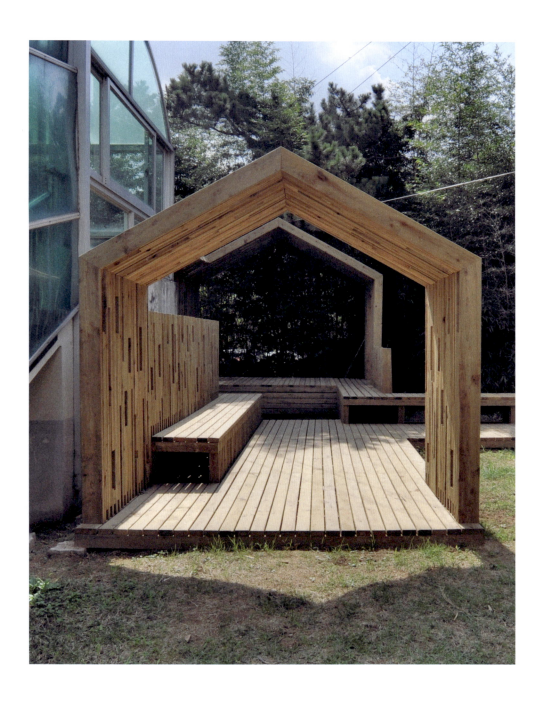

63

Shinmyeoung Daycare Center

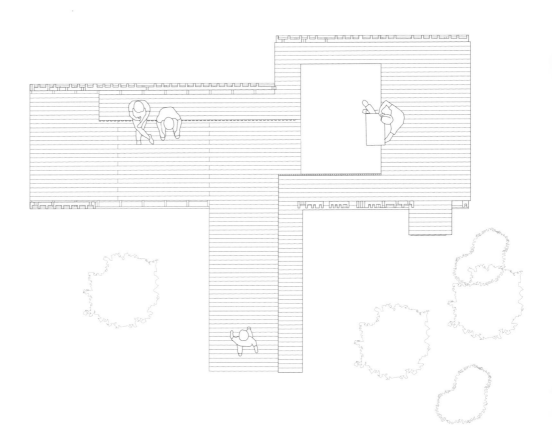

Garden

The pavilion was designed like a gabled house to give the impression of a secure and private space while also offering a stable and solid place for people to meet and talk to each other. Considering the surrounding context, the site was spatially divided into three sections according to different activities, including an entrance gate, a performing stage, and a gathering area. The entrance gate in the shape of a gabled frame welcomes visitors approaching the pavilion. The gabled roof's highest point is at 2.56 meters. A stage with a low wooden bench that is open to the yard is connected to the gate.

The ground was flattened and hardened to ensure that the blocks were laid out after a little groundwork to support the structure. They were laid on the block foundation and linked after weaving a set of lower floor joists. Each joist was cut with 2x4 lumbers and spaced approximately 42 centimeters apart. The top and lower floor joists were joined together. Floor plates and benches were placed at 5 millimeter intervals after the main structural frame for the wall and the roof were assembled. We decided that lumber was the most suitable material to use for this project because it is eco-friendly. Because the structure would be in close proximity to nature and used regularly by children, lumber also would allow for high-impact absorption so that children are able to run, play, and roll over on the deck.

Some wall and roof components that would be inserted between the main structures were formed on the spot without accurate sizes. Accordingly, different opening patterns for the walls and roofs were created. Children may peek inside and outside via the holes as the wind blows, and sunlight penetrates through the structure. The structural dimensions were simultaneously created considering anthropometric measures on infants and young children. Some areas where children sit and lie down were sanded back. Although it is common to apply a finish to components prior to the assembly, this time we added preservatives after the fabrication was completed. The lumbers were brushed with preservatives twice and then dried.

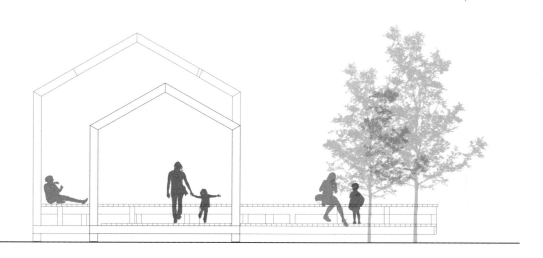

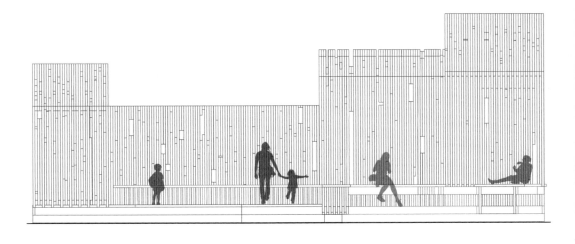

Program

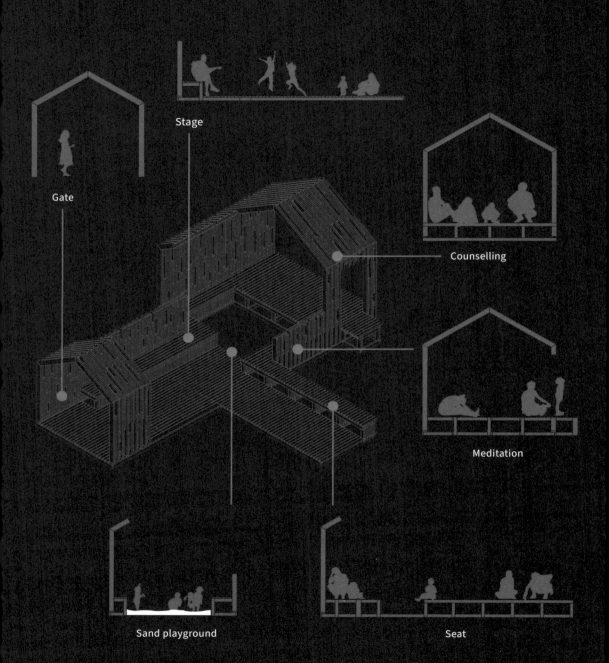

The stage is intended for performing or jumping around and is located at the innermost area of the pavilion. The gabled roof's highest point is at 3.57 meters. A portion of the roof has been taken away to allow sufficient natural light. The counselling and meditation spaces adjacent to the bamboo forest are intended to be a peaceful spot for children to rest, converse, and read books. Although we planned as such, children will use the pavilion in a variety of ways beyond our expectations. In addition, the pavilion may be used as a resting place for older people during school hours because the center also runs a nursing home.

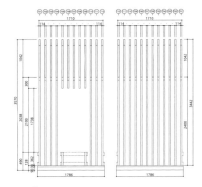

2x6 (24 pieces)

2x6 (6 pieces)

Wall components

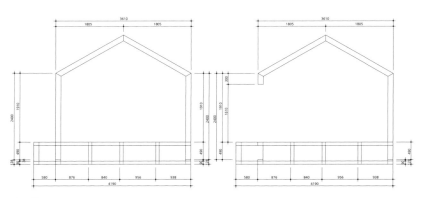

Sections

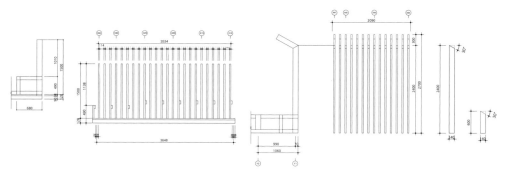

Wall and base components

Walls and roof

The roof and the wall are made of an integrated structure. The frame is fabricated with 2x6 lumbers, with 2x4 lumbers placed in between. The roof is made in the form of a gable with a 120-degree angle.

Floor and base

A set of lower and upper floor joists are laid, spaced approximately 420 millimeters apart. Then floors and benches are placed at intervals of 5 millimeters.

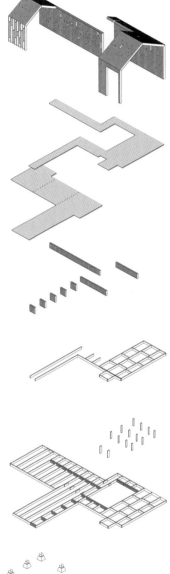

Concrete piers

Precast independent L-type concrete peer blocks are located at regular intervals in consideration of the load of the pavilion's upper structure.

71

Structural details

The main structural frame for the wall and the roof was fabricated with 2x6 dimensional lumbers, with 2x4 lumbers placed in between. The angle of the gabled roof frame was set at 120 degrees. This notion means that each roof component was sliced at a 30-degree angle. The gabled frame's peak joints are glued, clamped, and screwed at the frame joints.

The main structural sections of the floor, wall, and roof components were pre-assembled on site and piled up with stainless steel screws after cutting. Considering the lack of time and budget, we decided to attach each component one at a time rather than cut the grooves.

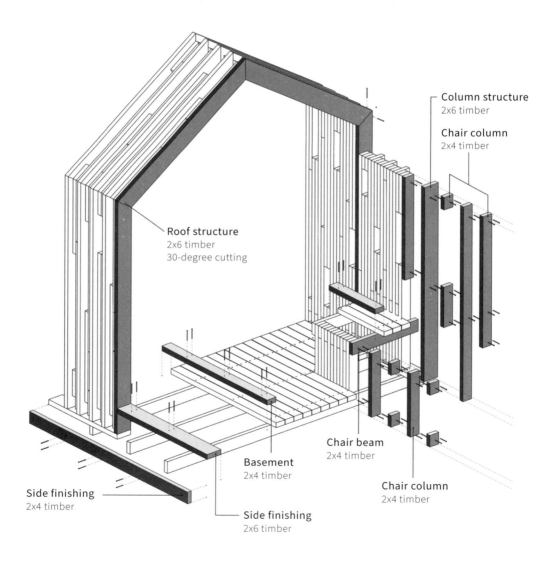

Playground axonometric

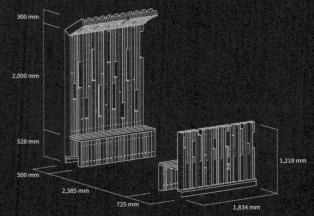

Entrance axonometric

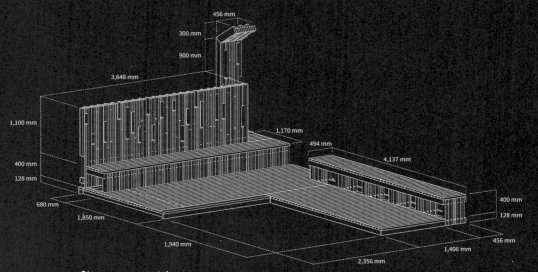

Stage axonometric

Study model

Study models effectively reveal potential design flaws early in the process. They provide valuable insights into the connections between various components, facilitating more efficient and accurate assembly, and thereby enhancing planning and decision-making during construction. Furthermore, these models contribute to a better understanding of load distribution and structural integrity, both of which are critical for ensuring safety and stability in the final structure.

Study model of Courtyard Hideout, scale 1:30

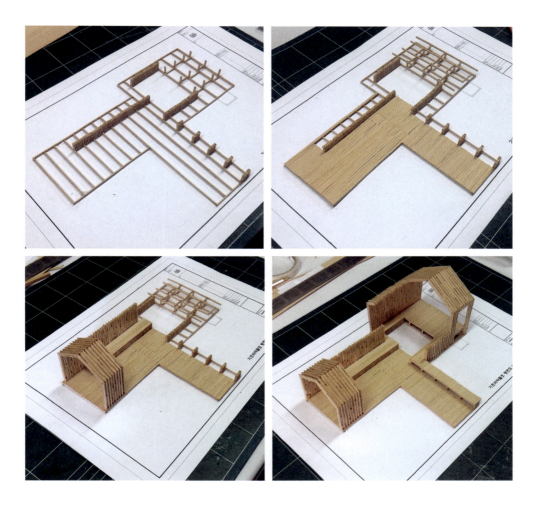

Lumbers of random and varied lengths fill the space between the vertical structures. A series of small holes ensure openness for visibility and bring in natural light and ventilation.

Spirit levels are used to ensure that construction components are aligned at the correct height.
A laser level is also used for leveling and aligning horizontal posts and base beams.

Some of the prefabricated units are assembled elsewhere on the site due to the limited work area and the constraints caused by various fabrication works.

Fifty students participated in the construction, which took five days to finish. The pavilion was donated to the center once it was completed, with all participants, donors, and children present. We imagine children sitting on the pavilion talking, practicing their instruments, drawing, or painting.

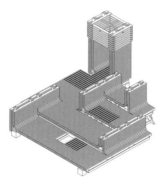

Cascading Grounds

Pine Tree Home
29 Ilshin-ro, Bupyeong-gu, Incheon, Korea
2016

The Embassy of Canada to Korea supported the initiative to design an outdoor wooden pavilion for children at the Pine Tree Home nursery center in Incheon, Korea. The Street Pavilion that was constructed in front of the embassy a few years earlier had a favorable impact on this sponsorship. Canada Wood Korea provided technical assistance and resources.

Besides residential facilities, the center lacks amenities for children. It is difficult to suitably meet the requirements and individual needs of each child and hard to consider their individual privacy.

According to a survey of local nursing centers, Pine Tree Home had the least facilities for children, despite the high proportion of young children and toddlers compared to other children's care facilities in Incheon. When queried about the possibility of a pavilion, the center expressed a strong desire, emphasizing the dire necessity for one.

The pavilion design was inspired by the concept of a playground where children may sit and play with their nannies and teachers while feeling secure in an intimate, grassy garden setting. A trail runs across the garden, and the pavilion was designed to naturally connect to the trail between the existing trees. Accessibility was addressed by installing the pavilion on the main route from the facility to the lawn. The design was developed in collaboration with architect Youngsoo Kim from More Less Architects and graduate students from D-Lab. The project's final construction was carried out by fifty architectural students who volunteered to help.

Step 1

Divide the ground

Step 2

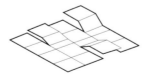

Lift the ground

Step 3

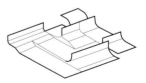

Create U-shaped deck

A view of the sky from the bottom of the tower

Yard wall

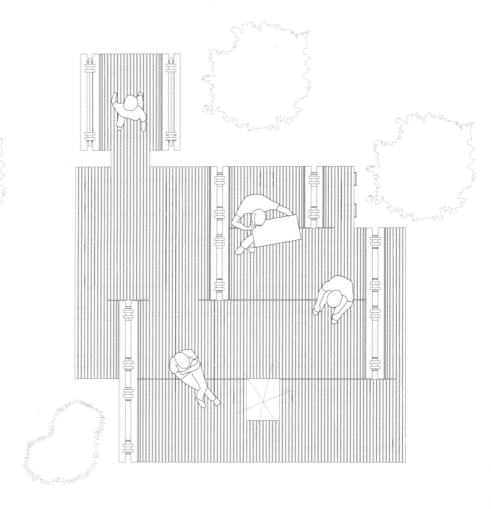

Wooden walkway

Children engage in social activities as they play in the pavilion.

Outdoor places, in addition to the residential accommodation where children live together are important areas that can support children's individual activities and positively impact their psychological and emotional stability. An outdoor pavilion in childcare facilities can provide a place for children to run around and be a great source of vitality fostering their growth.

Based on this concept, we designed a pavilion in the facility's side yard to inspire children's creativity. The initial design was prepared through several conceptual sketches and study models to embody the ideas envisioned. A number of decks are designed to encourage diverse social interactions among children by freely crossing with tiers of cascading grounds that recur at four different levels. Hence, children can sit at different eye levels to converse with friends. The width of the plates gradually decreases with the slight increase in height.

The floor plates were woven into low side walls to create a seamless curve. Multiple layers of U-shaped decking appear to repeatedly flow. A tiny tower was designed as an object on the back of the plates, giving it a distinct sense of vertical space. Shrubs and towering trees, along with the pavilion, provide a changing mood of time and seasons. Looking through an open roof was designed to give children the impression of peering through a telescope into the sky. It was also conceived as a memory picture frame, encouraging children to remember their childhood sky by framing the scene like a photograph.

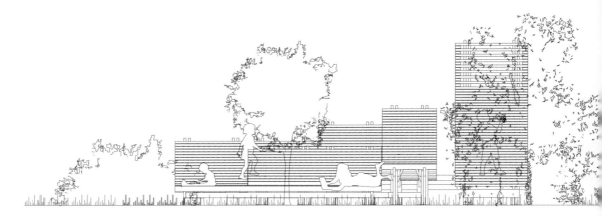

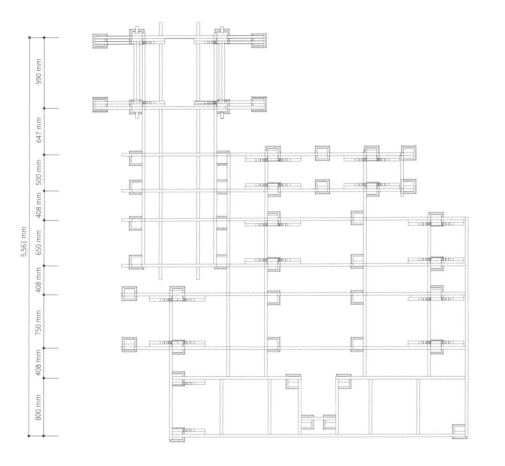

Foundation layout

Deck and tower
Deck plates and deck and tower walls are constructed with 2x4 SPF lumbers

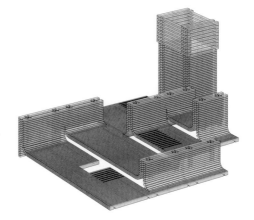

Structure
Lower floor joists, columns, and the supporting frames of the curved sections are constructed with 2x6 SPF lumbers

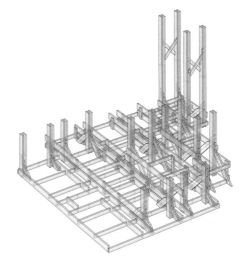

Concrete piers
The foundation is built with concrete pier blocks

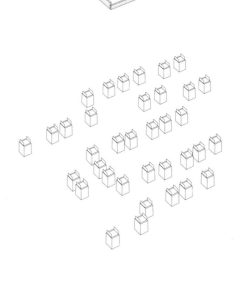

Laser-cut pieces for the study model

CNC router for fabricating scale study model at the Gwacheon National Science Museum.

Structural assembly

Three different sizes of dimensional lumbers, including 2x4 and 2x6 SPF lumbers, were used for the pavilion structure. We found that the material is more suited to nursery facilities than other materials because children can freely run and play due to its high shock-absorption rate. They were pre-incised before cutting for efficient preservative treatment. The 2x6 lumber was used for lower floor joists and columns, while the 2x4 lumber was used to construct deck plates and walls. The 2x6 lumber was also used for the supporting frames of the curved sections that smoothly connect deck plates. The grooves in these supporting frames were cut with a CNC milling machine. Accordingly, the deck lumbers can slot snugly in this groove and are then secured with stainless steel screws.

To efficiently create the curved decks, we inserted the narrow side of the 2x4 lumber into the joists. Then the lumbers were cut with grooves and coupled to the joist on the floor. We cut approximately forty percent of the component depth for the grooves for floor stability. The lumber was installed with 20-millimeter-wide gap between each piece to allow it to naturally warp and expand with the weather. The deck lumbers were then fixed with stainless steel screws on each joist. More lumber was required to achieve the desired outcome than would be used for a normal deck in which 2x4 wood is typically laid horizontally, reducing the amount of wood required.

Study model of a curved section of Cascading Grounds, scale 1:1

Study model

Various study models were used throughout the process to examine intricate joinery and structural durability. After the design was completed, all the components were precisely cut according to the designs and sequentially preassembled by the students to ensure the accuracy of the construction. The groove positions of each component were identified after the lumbers were cut to match the length of each component, and the grooves were cut with appropriate diameters and depths. The trimmer was used to cut the grooves, and the finishing work was carried out by hand with chisels. Appropriate screw holes were dug out in advance to allow the preservative to penetrate.

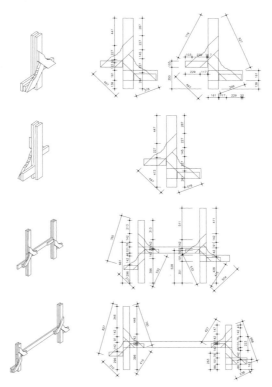

Diagonal brace on the sides of the deck to tie posts to joists

Study model materials and equipment

After marking the exact assembly positions of each component, they were divided into groups, tied together, and transported to the factory for antiseptic treatment. We paid particular attention to the treatment because this pavilion would be installed outside. The ACQ preservative treatment was applied twice. Then the wood was cured for one week to preserve the lumber exterior long term. Meanwhile, the tools were organized in the order in which they would be needed, and other hardware was ordered according to the predetermined assembly. Students were assigned to various stages of the construction process. During this time, we became aware that some participating students had little to no experience using tools. Experts from Canada Wood Korea led them through a day of training to teach them how to use the tools and treat the materials.

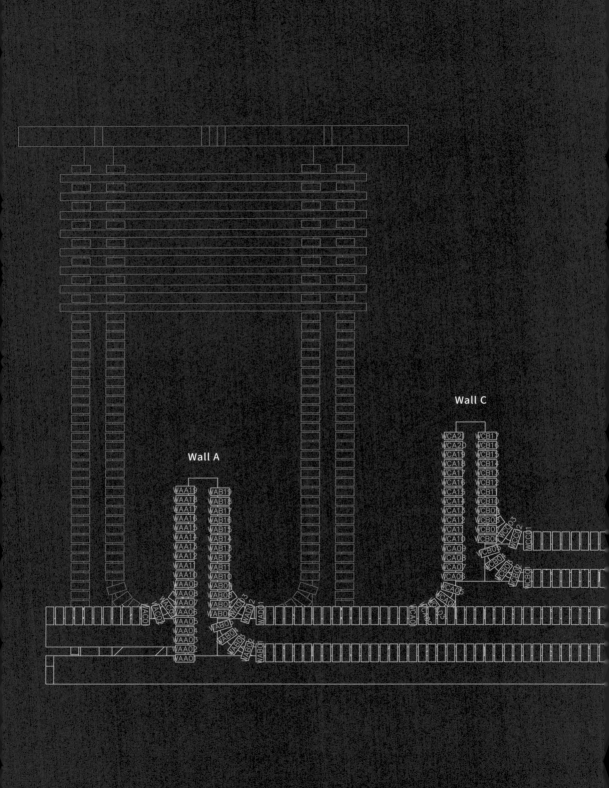

Wall A

A01-09 (09EA): 38x89x1,200 mm
A10-19 (10EA): 38x89x2,358 mm
B01-09 (09EA): 38x89x1,200 mm
B10-19 (10EA): 38x89x2,358 mm
C01-05 (05EA) : 38x89x1,050 mm
D01-05 (05EA) : 38x89x900 mm

Wall B

A01-09 (09EA): 38x89x1,150 mm
A10-12 (03EA): 38x89x2,208 mm
B01-16 (16EA): 38x89x2,208 mm
C01-05 (05EA): 38x89x1,050 mm

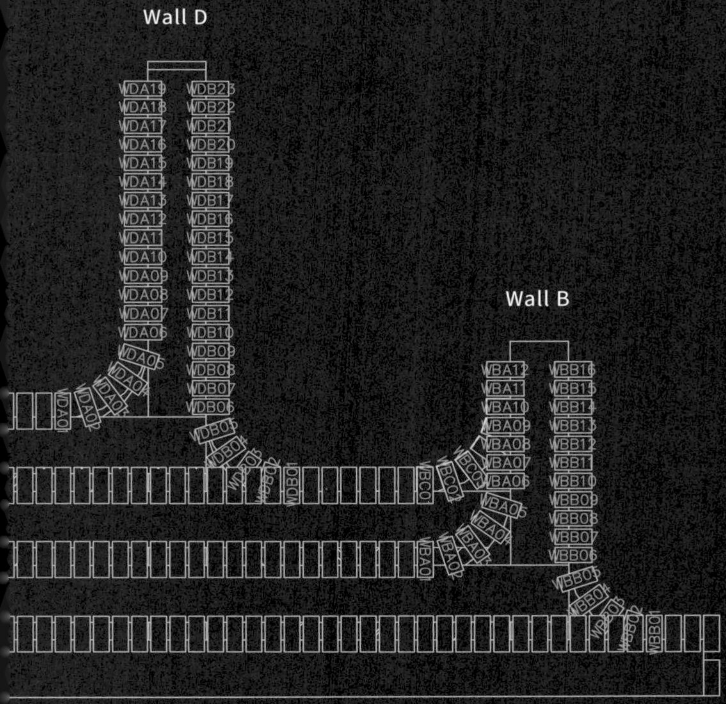

Wall C

A01-21 (21EA): 38x89x1,958 mm
B01-09 (09EA): 38x89x1,050 mm
B10-17 (08EA): 38x89x1,200 mm
C01-05 (05EA): 38x89x900 mm

Wall D

A01-19 (19EA): 38x89x900 mm
B01-23 (23EA): 38x89x900 mm

The sequential design displays the rigor of repetition and pattern of linear elements demonstrated in works by Sol LeWitt, Frank Stella, Ian Davenport, Bridget Riley, and Sean Scully. The design is based on the repetition of a standard 2x4 lumber. While the unit does not alter its fundamental form, it appears to vary by the way in which units are severed and recomposed.

Concrete pier blocks are placed for the foundation. The placement preserves two existing trees and bushes on the site.

We cleaned out the bushes and pruned tree branches that were hanging over the structure. Working the design around existing trees serves as the glue that holds the design together and keeps the beauty of the landscape intact. During the construction, large holes were made in the floor to allow the trees to grow. The trees eventually became the natural roof of this pavilion, shielding it from the harsh sunlight.

We used 240-by-260-by-220-millimeter concrete pier blocks for the foundation. The ground was dug out to a depth of 200 millimeters and the pier blocks were lined up on the right positions. A laser level kit was used to adjust the height of the pier blocks. Several blocks were grouped together and cement was poured on the bottom to secure them. After the cement dried, the concrete blocks were covered with soil.

Once all the components were delivered to the site, they were organized according to the assembly. Columns and joists were installed on the pier blocks with 2x6 lumbers. The columns, joists, and beams were tightly connected to ensure safety and stability because there were various levels of the floor plates. After the underfloor structure was completed, the floor plates were covered with 2x4 and fixed with stainless steel screws. After completing the fabrication, shrubs were planted around the structure and soft woodchips were placed around the pavilion to reduce the children's risk of injury if they fall.

During the four-month preparation period, students took time to come up with unique ideas and detailed solutions even though they were in the middle of the semester. Assembling the pavilion took almost a week with fifty participating students, including graduate and undergraduate architectural students. Upon completion, individual volunteers, donors, recipients, and supporters gathered to celebrate the pavilion being donated to Pine Tree Home. The Canadian embassy also donated school and household supplies to the center. This structure is the result of the effort and support of many students and donors. We see this pavilion as a one-of-a-kind outdoor place for the children to play and somewhere they may form childhood memories.

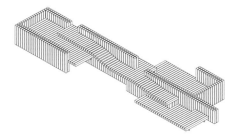

Blooming Landscape

Onsaemiro Flower Road
1736-13 Sillim-dong, Gwanak-gu, Seoul, Korea
2017

The Blooming Landscape project was proposed by D-Lab and implemented with the cooperation of the neighborhood residents. It was funded by the Seoul Metropolitan Government and sponsored by Gwanak-gu District Office. The project was located on the Onsaemiro Flower Road next to the Nanhyang Elementary School in Sillim-dong, Gwanak-gu, Seoul. The area was originally part of a stream where water flowed down from the mountain. Although it was covered with irrigation and reclaimed land, the ground was still weak. In the past it had been used as a parking lot and illegal dumping site for construction waste, resulting in continuous complaints about the degradation of the area's beauty and the smell produced by the neglected garbage.

Since then, residents in the neighborhood had gathered to transform the abandoned area into a flower garden. Residents had continually requested that the Gwanak-gu District Office build a shelter because there was no resting place in the garden. After consultation with the Seoul Metropolitan Government, we decided to create a pavilion for the neighborhood. The area was deemed to be the most appropriate place for our continuing effort toward the "pavilions for giving" project. Architect Minwook Choi from Smaller Architects joined the project in collaboration with D-Lab.

The chosen site measures approximately 770.6 square meters. The pavilion is only a 9-by-3-meter area sandwiched between the retaining wall of the elementary school and the 28-meter-wide front road. The property had a long sloping path across the site. We considered creating a natural deck to connect the upper and lower levels of the garden that could be used by anyone moving along the path. There is an elementary school and a day care center nearby; hence, children could use it as a safe way to do to and from the school. The pavilion could also be used as a relaxing place for the large population of senior citizens in the area.

Step 1

Establish the longitudinal axis with slopes

Step 2

Determine the territorial boundaries

Step 3

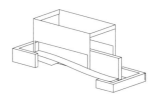

Add the upper structure

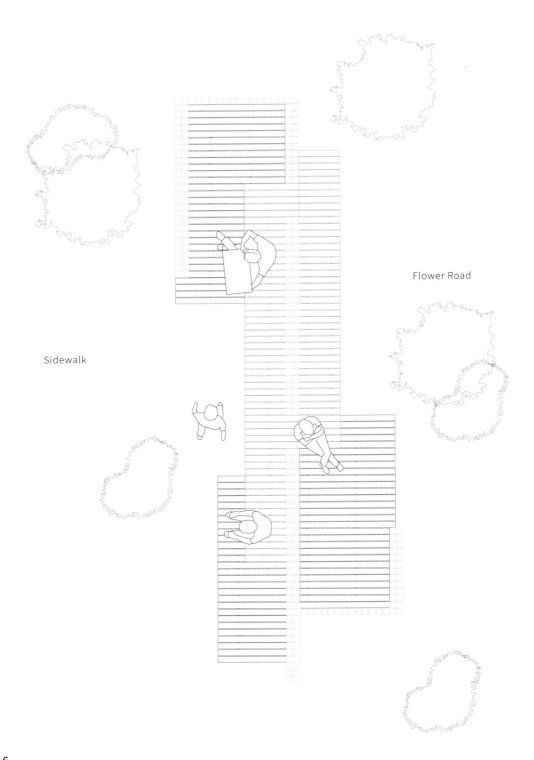

Several decks of various heights were placed as close to the sloped land as possible. People can take advantage of the pavilion as a multipurpose activity area. Low walls were also designed to divide the realm of activities and allow for multiple groups to get together. Meanwhile, people can sit on top of the low walls or various levels of decking, or lean against the walls to rest and enjoy the surrounding flower beds.

There is a safety and maintenance issue because the pavilion will be installed in an open public area where an unspecified number of people can enjoy it at anytime. We decided to use 4x4 lumbers for the structure to ensure the most durable and bulky materials with the minimum number of components. After conducting several design experiments through a series of structure models, a design was selected that illustrates the simple repetitive rhythm of vertical and horizontal bands of lumber.

The size of the lumber was used as an expressive tool for visual order and aesthetic unity in the final design. The components and their connection joints are accurately drawn for the precision of the construction. The assembly process was simulated through computer visualization and mock-up models. Thereafter, the number of lumbers needed was calculated and ordered. Hardware, tools, and other equipment were prepared.

Structural assembly

We were concerned with uneven settlement caused by the sinking of the structure foundation because it is installed in a sloping area that is a landfill. To prevent uneven settlement due to differences in load size and irregularities of the foundation during the construction, the foundation structure was united as a single structure to equalize the load of the upper structure. Consequently, an integrated substructure using metal pipes was designed for the independent foundation. All metal frames were predesigned and cut on-site, and the components were welded together. The construction was carried out in the winter; hence, the frozen land was hard to deal with. After, the ground was dug out as much as necessary using an excavator. The ground was leveled, and L-shaped independent piers were positioned and fixed in the correct place. This process took two days.

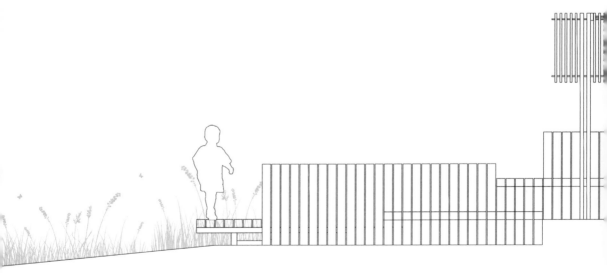

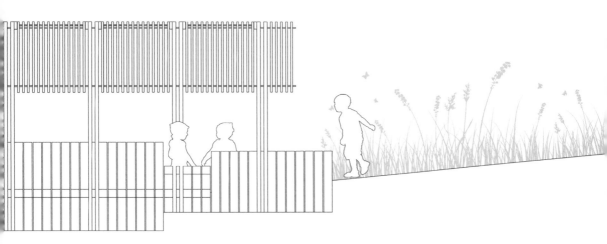

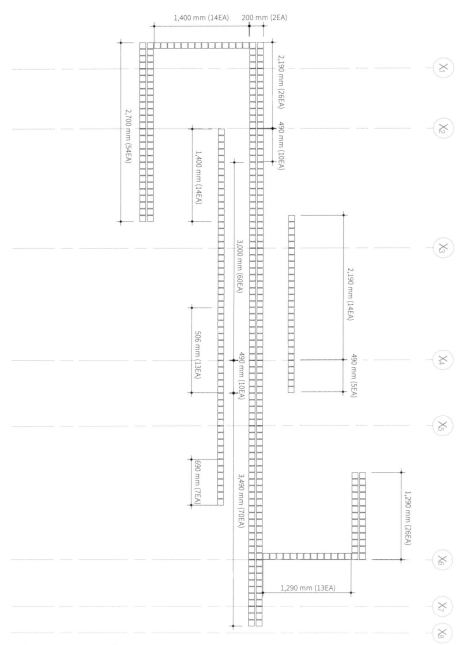

Column component layout

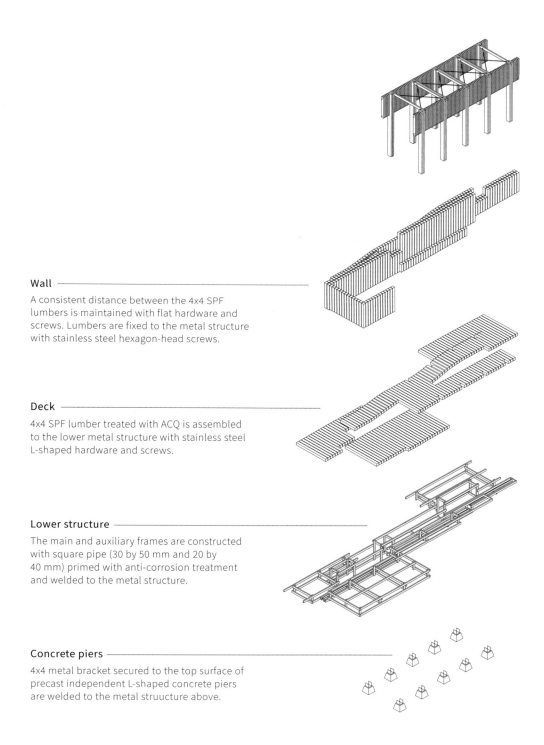

Wall

A consistent distance between the 4x4 SPF lumbers is maintained with flat hardware and screws. Lumbers are fixed to the metal structure with stainless steel hexagon-head screws.

Deck

4x4 SPF lumber treated with ACQ is assembled to the lower metal structure with stainless steel L-shaped hardware and screws.

Lower structure

The main and auxiliary frames are constructed with square pipe (30 by 50 mm and 20 by 40 mm) primed with anti-corrosion treatment and welded to the metal structure.

Concrete piers

4x4 metal bracket secured to the top surface of precast independent L-shaped concrete piers are welded to the metal struucture above.

Roof structure

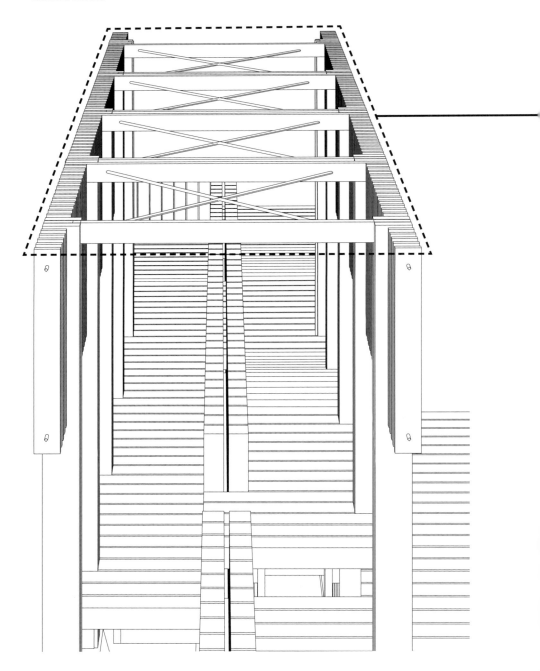

The original concept was for the roof structure to have vine plants grow within the stainless steel wire mesh and provide shade.

The slope of the entire site is a 12-degree angle in a longitudinal axis. It extends from north to south along the retaining wall of an elementary school to the west. The structure was constructed with a series of horizontal plates of different heights along the long path, leveraging the slope. A roof structure was planned to obtain visual recognition of the structure and to provide a shaded area because there is neither device nor tree to offer shade for the whole facility. Accordingly, vine trees growing along a wire mesh in the middle of the roof structure were intended to provide shade. However, during the district office's design review, the committee recommended removing the roof structure for safety reasons, so it was eliminated from the final design.

Study model of Blooming Landscape, scale 1:20

Study model

This study model is crucial for understanding the positioning of the peer base and the details of the lower metal structure. It offers more specific insights into structural reliability and the appropriate types of joint connections compared to digital models, making potential instabilities and weaknesses more apparent. Additionally, this study model helps identify the precise locations of bolts and nuts for connecting the upper and lower structures, as well as joists and columns, highlighting the need for various metal brackets.

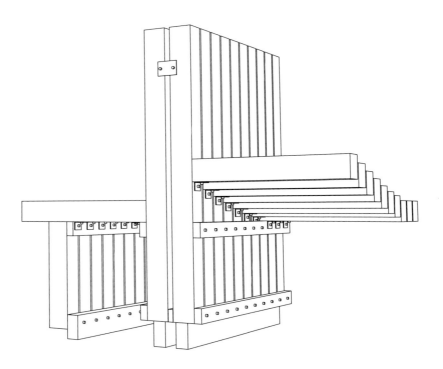

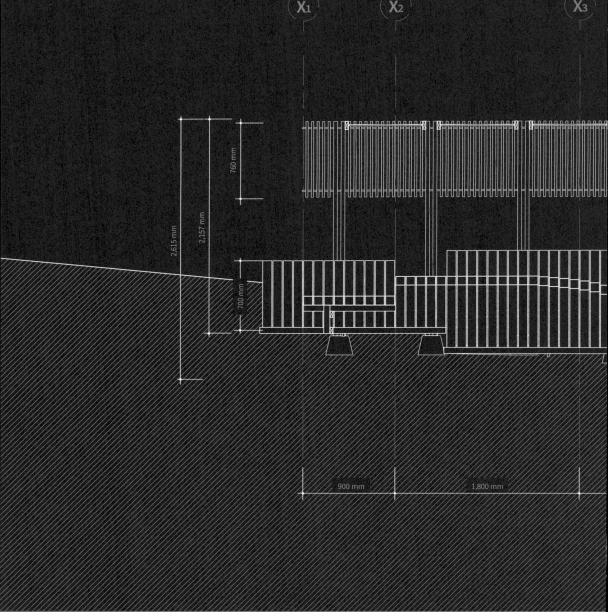

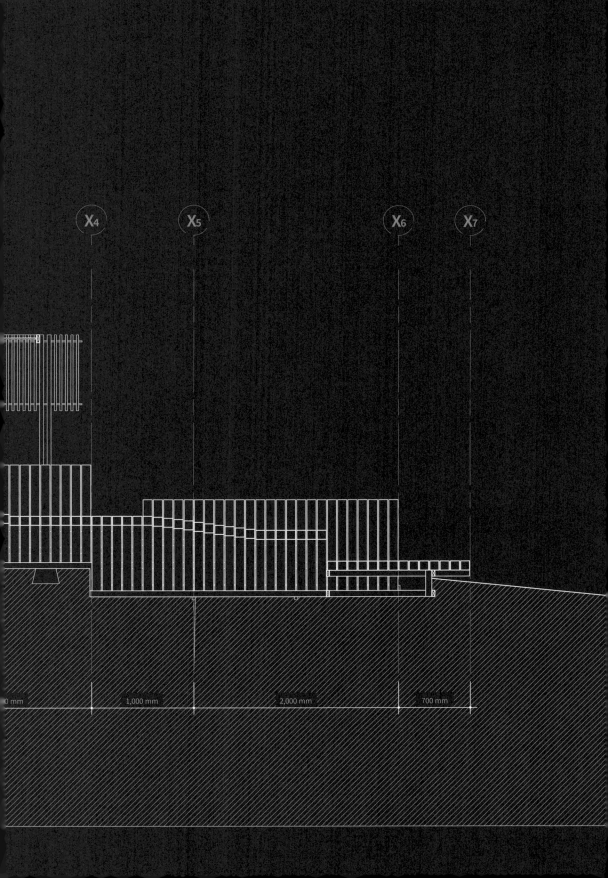

Large piles of scrap timber in random shapes and sizes lay around the site. We developed ideas to use the timber efficiently, including simple box chairs for use in the pavilion.

Dimensional lumber with 4x4 ACQ incised Douglas fir

A foundation frame made with square pipes was installed on top of the piers. Square pipe 30 by 50 millimeters in size was used for the main structure and 20 by 40 millimeters for the auxiliary frame, primed with rust prevention. The process of fabricating and assembling structures, including cutting and welding, has many safety issues for students; hence, experts were employed to assist. All metal frame components were cut and welded on-site and firmly connected to the independent piers. After welding the frame, the ground was well stomped with dirt in case of uneven settlement in the spring. Once the structure was completed, the land was compacted again several times with an excavator.

Each 4x4 lumber component was cut on-site. The process was straightforward and relatively easy due to the absence of grooves needed for the construction. The components were assembled to the metal substructure using L-shaped hardware and stainless steel self-tapping screws. Flat hardware was also used to maintain a consistent distance between the components that were then fixed with stainless steel direct screws. The upper structure and deck components were assembled with a gap of 5 millimeters between them, to allow the lumber to expand and contract in the weather throughout the year. There was a continuous process of inserting and fixing the members into the substructure in order.

Although the pavilion design was simple in form, we encountered several difficulties during construction. It was carried out in the snowy winter; hence, the moisture caused the lumbers to severely warp. A series of assembly problems occurred when aligning the horizontal and vertical position of the components. When installing the lumber into the lower metal substructure, the size of the components did not fit due to the dampened lumber. We re-cut them several times to fit the metal frame. After assembly was complete, the structure was coated twice with an eco-friendly oil stain preservative on a warm, sunny day when it was able to dry.

Flat hardware maintains a consistent distance between the components.

The residents wanted landscaping around the pavilion to include trees that would provide shade year-round while highlighting the beauty of the changing seasons. This included fruit trees, ginkgo trees, and pine trees donated by a private business.

A detailed fabrication plan was prepared with a full set of drawings. An action plan to source and receive materials according to the process was prepared in advance. More than twenty students participated in the construction and completed the pavilion fabrication over the course of three weeks. Neighborhood residents stopped by the jobsite every day and watched the whole process. Some residents helped us with cleaning and gardening after the pavilion was completed. During the construction, they offered snacks or warm tea. After overcoming various difficulties, the pavilion was finalized and donated to the residents. Satisfaction levels with the pavilion were high across households living around the garden. The project received a Seoul Creativity Award from the Seoul Metropolitan Government in recognition of the design creativity, residents' participation, social contribution, and talent-sharing activities.

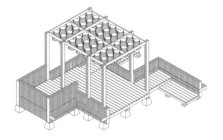

Bucket Pavilion

Star of the Sea Children's Home
15 Inha-ro 91beon-gil, Michuhol-gu, Incheon
2018

The Bucket Pavilion project was sponsored by the USUN, Korea. It consists of a pavilion at the Star of the Sea Children's Home, Incheon. The home was established to care for and nurture children from birth to six years old who are left without a parent or guardian for various reasons. The Catholic social welfare facility is operated by nuns and protects children before adoption. According to the head of the home, small recreation facilities and gardens are well maintained, but there is a lack of outdoor facilities for infants and children to be exposed to sunlight to boost their immunity and growth. Above all, the home should provide dedicated, individual attention from steady caregivers, otherwise there can be serious effects on the emotional, mental, and social development of children, especially those under the age of six years.

For this reason, we decided to design an outdoor pavilion in the neglected area between the nursery playground and the garden where rocks, trees, and bushes are located. The construction was conducted by professional architects from the project's sponsor, in collaboration with architectural students.

The project was carried out by designing a sun-filled shelter around the trees with consideration to the body size of infants and children aged zero to six years. The unique characteristics of the structure include several levels of decking at various heights to allow caregivers to wander through the pavilion with their children and babies and to sit on the benches. Access routes were planned in relation to the movement of playing in the neighboring playground and garden.

Star of the Sea Children's Home building

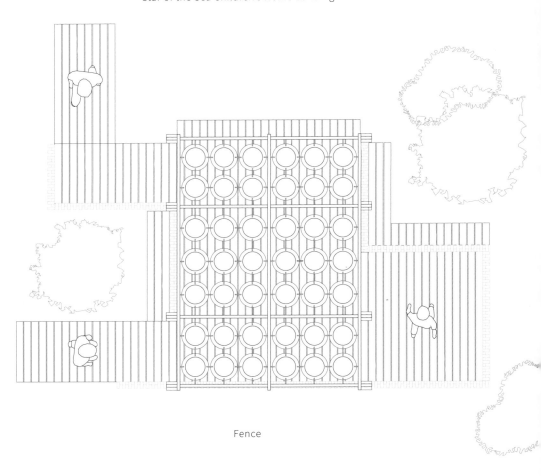

Fence

Hanging metal buckets

The project aims to provide the children with a special experience and memory. Instead of installing a regular roof, we decided to hang metal buckets upside down and paint the inside of the buckets. Galvanized buckets were used to prevent corrosion and rust. Wires were weaved through holes on the sides of the buckets to hang them on the roof structure. The buckets will make natural sounds during different weather, such as when it rains or the wind blows. On the sunny days, children will be exposed to sunlight beaming through the gaps between the buckets. Students, children, and caregivers collaborated on the project by painting various colors, shapes, and designs inside the buckets. The process triggered the interest of the children.

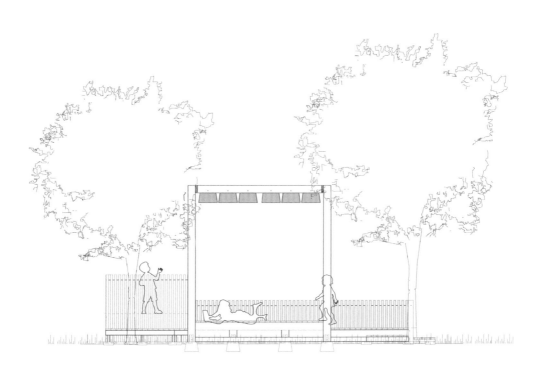

After the components were cut, each one was numbered with pens and relocated around the site in the correct order of assembly. In some other projects, we transported the components to a factory for ACQ preservative treatment, but because of the lack of budget for this project, students instead painted each component twice with eco-friendly oil stain preservatives. One group cut the components, while the other group placed L-shaped independent piers on the site, adjusting the height of the pier level evenly.

The 2x2, 2x4, and 2x6 SPF lumbers were used for this pavilion. The columns, roof beams, and main flooring joists are 2x6 SPF lumbers installed with auxiliary hardware. The 2x4 components were sandwiched between each 2x6 and tightened together to create the columns connecting the floor joists and roof beams. The main parts of the columns and joists were fixed with a stainless steel hexagon-head bolt with a thickness of 6 millimeters and a length of 55 millimeters. The 2x2 and 2x4 lumber was alternately placed to give the wall a sense of rhythm and even out the gaps between the 2x4 components. Once the wall components were cut, they were drilled 10 millimeters into the correct position and connected using 8-millimeter-diameter steel-threaded rods and tightened with stainless steel nuts. After the wall modules were placed, the floor deck was installed using 2x4 lumbers.

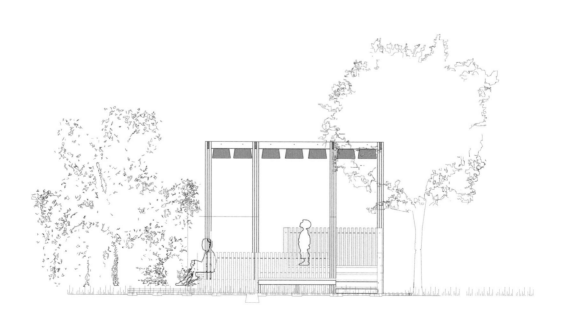

Plan and elevation drawings of wall components

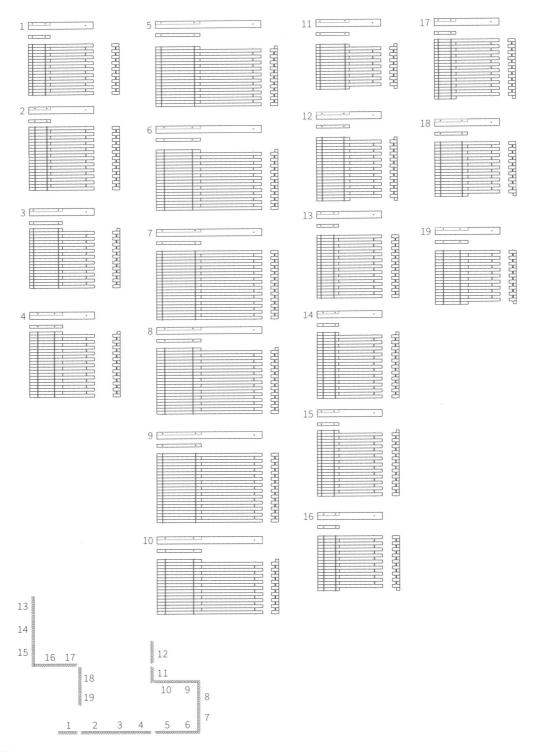

Roof

Galvanized buckets were threaded with stainless steel wire rope and hung on stainless steel iron cable. The inside of the buckets was painted with oil paints.

Structural frame

The frame is assembled with 2x4 and 2x6 lumber treated with oil stain preservative and fixed with stainless steel screws.

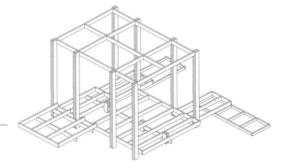

Walls and deck

The walls and deck are 2x2 and 2x4 SPF lumbers. The wall components are connected with stainless steel threaded rods and washers.

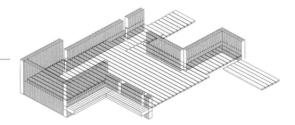

Concrete piers

Precast independent L-shaped concrete piers have metal brackets secured to the top surface of the pier.

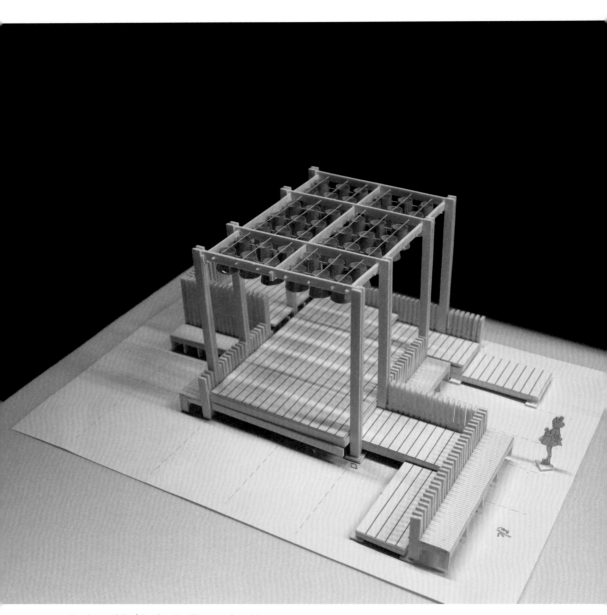
Study model of Bucket Pavilion, scale 1:20

Study model

A number of mock-up models were fabricated as the design was being developed. We also discussed the designs with the nuns. After the final design was approved, each component was drawn for accurate cutting purposes. During the process, unexpected details and joinery were completely resolved. Each component was accurately cut by participating students with table saws. After the components for the walls were cut to fit the length of each lumber, the locations of 10-millimeter-diamete steel-threaded rods were marked to drill holes. The grooves were cut where necessary for the roof structure.

This mock-up set out to test how to properly install and hang the galvanized buckets upside down to the roof frame with a 3.14-millimeter-diameter iron cable. Stainless steel eye hook screws were attached to the structural frame and wires were tied with wire rope clips. Pieces of 2x4 SPF lumber were combined at 2-inch-wide intervals with 10-millimeter-diameter stainless steel threaded rods. They were then fixed with 2-millimeter-thick washers with a 10 millimeter inner diameter and 20 millimeter outer diameter. All components of the model were at full scale.

Bucket mockup

For the roof, galvanized buckets measuring 350 millimeters in diameter and 325 millimeters in height were hung upside down. The exact locations of the hanging buckets were drilled in advance, and the inside of each bucket was painted with eco-friendly oil paints. After the first layer of gesso (a primer/white paint used to coat rigid surfaces) was applied, six basic colors were used on the inside. Once the paint had dried, the buckets were hung from the roof frame using a 3.14-millimeter-diameter iron cord, and the ends were fixed using an eye nut and wire clip. After the structure was completed, it was coated twice with a water-based eco-friendly wood preservative.

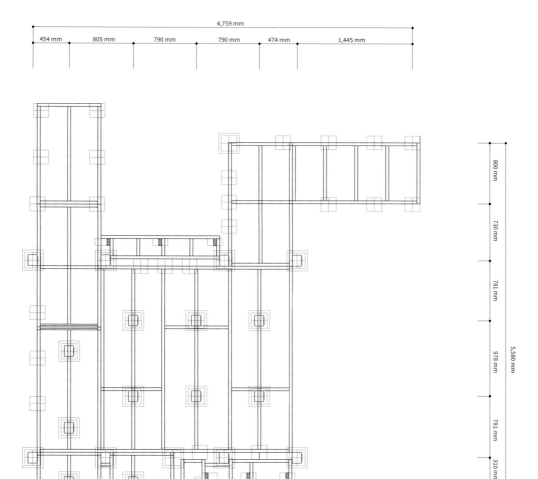

Foundation layout

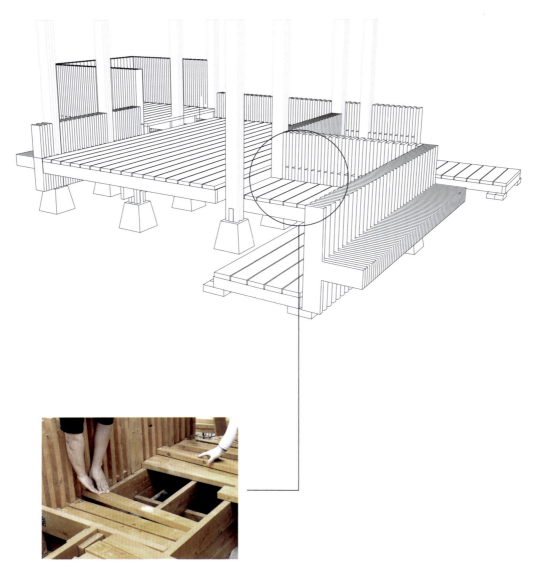

Each flooring component is spaced 2 inches apart, secured with a 6-millimeter thick, 55-millimeter long stainless steel hexagon head bolt, along with a stainless steel nut that has an 8-millimeter internal diameter and a 13-millimeter external diameter.

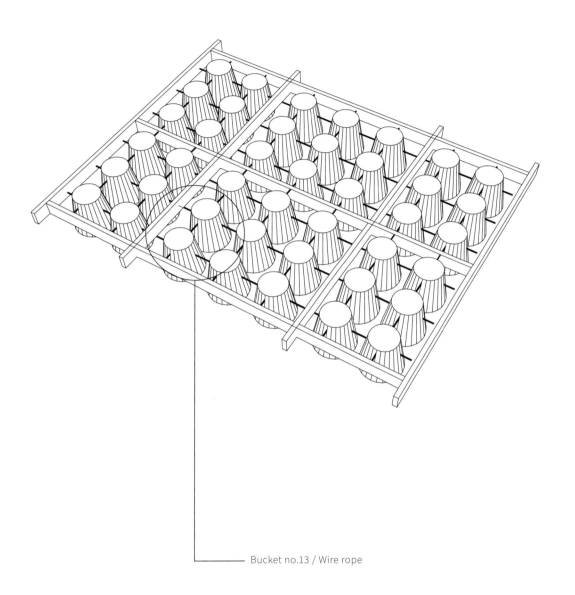

Bucket no.13 / Wire rope

The insides of the buckets were painted with an array of colors. Painting is an excellent activity for children to express their creativity. Using different colors, they can express themselves without words.

After digging the ground, the concrete piers are placed in the correct position.

Stacked lumbers for the walls are connected and screwed together

More than sixty people, including thirty architects from USUN Engineering and thirty students, participated to complete the construction in five days. The foundation work was carried out over two days and the assembly of components took three days. Upon completion, the pavilion was donated to the center with all participant donors, nuns, caregivers, and children present. Some leftover materials were passed on to the nursery manager for future maintenance of the pavilion, along with relevant information about how to maintain the pavilion. We like to imagine children running under the green trees, jumping, and resting on the pavilion with their friends, laughing happily. Although children will be able to read books and play around in the pavilion, they will also be proud when they look up at the paintings inside the buckets. It will be a place to make happy memories.

The insides of the buckets are colorfully painted, providing the children with a great way to channel their creativity.

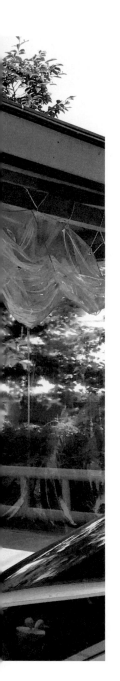
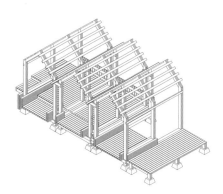

Seoksu Community Pavilion

13-8 Anyang-ro 532beon-gil
Anyang-si, Gyeonggi-do, Korea
2019

The Seoksu Community Pavilion project was implemented through the close collaboration of D-Lab and Canada Wood Korea, with the co-sponsorship of the province of Alberta, Canada, and the city of Anyang, Korea. The purpose was to construct a pavilion and donate it to the community. The senior population in the neighborhood of Seoksu 2-dong, Anyang, is rapidly aging. The area is full of low-income dwellings and townhouses that also lack community facilities for residents. After several discussions and site visits with the Urban Regeneration Division of Anyang City, some potential sites for a pavilion were chosen. Upon consideration of various conditions, a site was selected for the design development. The area around the site features not only poor public facilities but also inadequate parking lots, narrow roads, and a substantial amount of trash and household waste everywhere.

The site is located between an ordinary sidewalk and a stream, occupying a small area measuring 8 by 4 square meters. The site already has an existing pavilion with an old and mediocre design. Although it was intended to be a community gathering place in an open space, it is currently used as a shabby shelter. The poorly designed and maintained pavilion continues to negatively influence the character of the surrounding area. We proposed a better design with abundant architectural imagination to positively revive the bleak and gloomy atmosphere of the area and to appeal to all local residents across generations.

Researchers from D-Lab experimented with a few designs before settling on a final one for development. The selected design resembles a cluster of houses that can offer comfort and warmth for the neighboring residents. The basic design of the pavilion caters to passing pedestrians who may sit and rest on decks along the walkway. It was expected to become a community gathering space for all ages by installing various levels of horizontal decks. To escape from the existing dark ceiling, the roof was installed with translucent polycarbonate to create a lively and bright atmosphere in the pavilion.

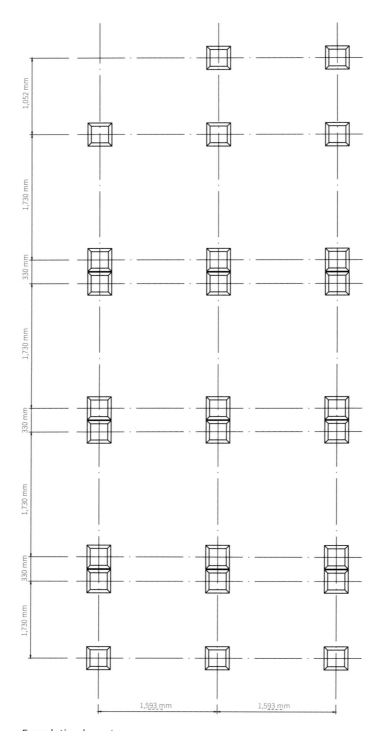

Foundation layout

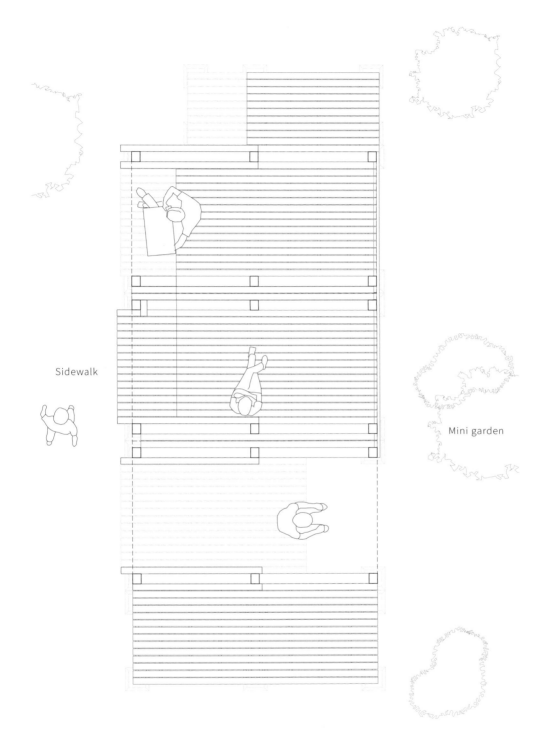

Structural assembly

SPF dimensional lumbers were used for the component manufacturing and lumber was pre-incised for chemical treatment. The 2x6 lumber was used for the main structural framework, such as columns, rafters, and joists. The joining part of column components and rafters was cut on a 45-degree angle to form a clean gabled design. Meanwhile, 2x4 lumber was used for the decks. Some components were grooved for structural stability.

Each set of components was fabricated off-site, cut according to the size and location of the components, and numbered for accurate assembly. Depending on the usage characteristics of each member, the letters S (structure), D (deck), W (wall), and R (roof) were written with numbers in sequence. Cutting and assembling each component with accurate sizes and precise positionings was extremely important for the completion of the pavilion. All components were organized like assembly kits and transported to the site after antiseptic treatment. The components were ACQ-treated for long-term use.

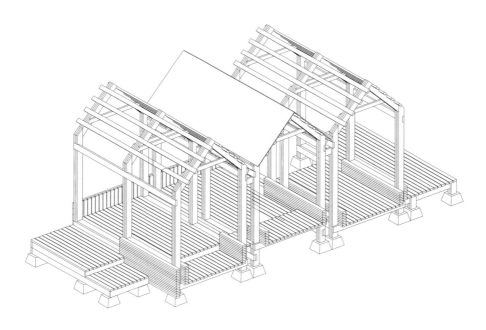

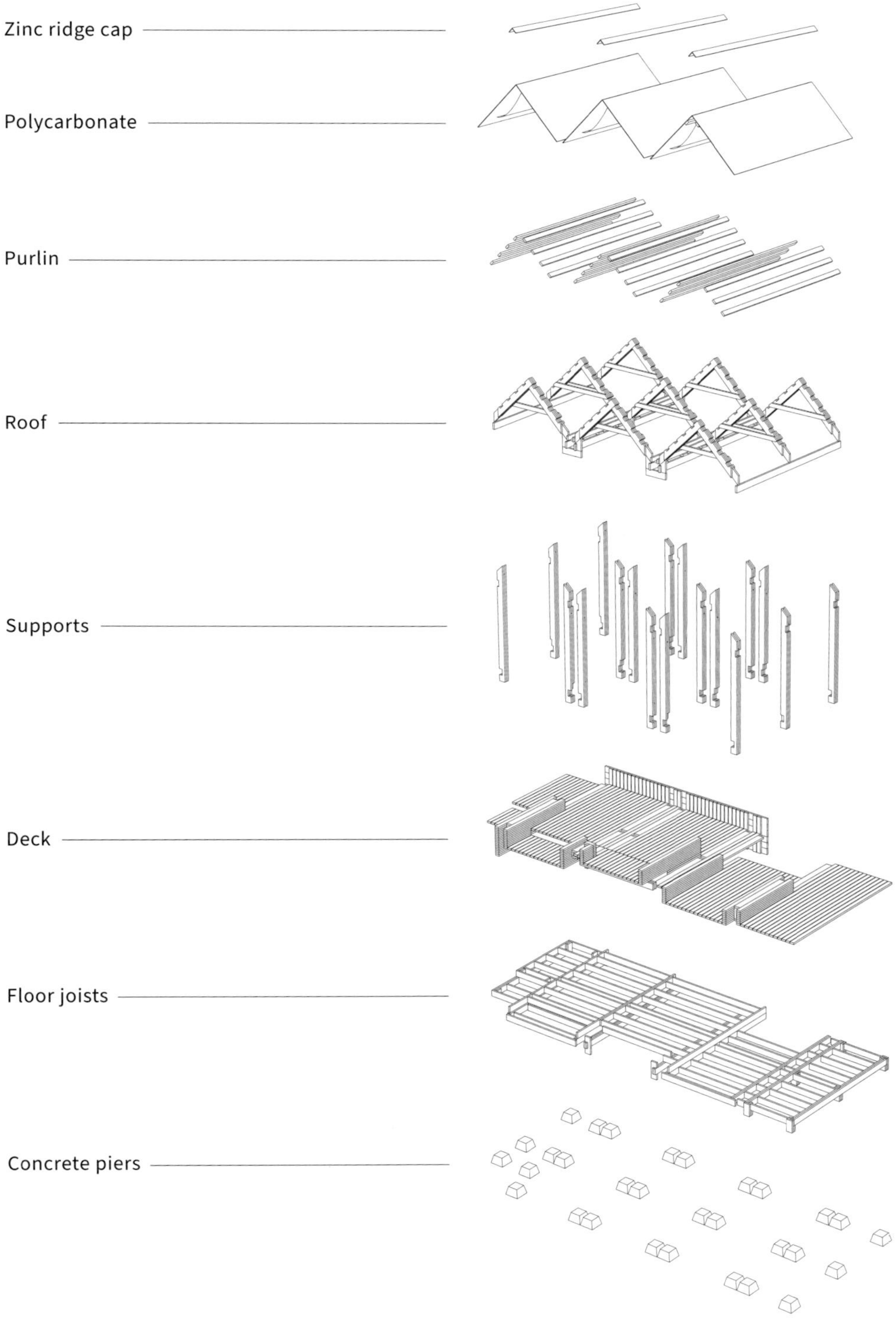

Zinc ridge cap

Polycarbonate

Purlin

Roof

Supports

Deck

Floor joists

Concrete piers

Study model of Seoksu Community Pavilion, scale 1:20

Study model

In developing the detailed design, various stages of mock-up models were constructed in scale 1:20 and tested to examine structural details, joinery, finishes, stability, and safety. Once the design was finalized, the components were separated to determine exact sizes and shapes and to demonstrate how the components fit together to achieve an optimal assembly of the structure. The scaled model of the design was fabricated out of inexpensive materials and used to evaluate design elements and work out details that are best visualized using a physical three-dimensional model. Comparisons were undertaken between the physical scale models and the computer simulation models to check any errors. The students presented the final design option to the surrounding neighbors and city administrative officers to give them the opportunity to share their feedback on the design. Several changes were made to meet the needs of the residents.

In the process of developing a series of detailed mock-up models, the assembly underwent extensive scrutiny. Precise drawings were created and the assembly of the components was animated using a computer program. Through this process, the completeness of the structure was enhanced and the assembly process was planned step by step. The technical support from Canada Wood Korea was helpful when solving problems and confirming other details of the structure.

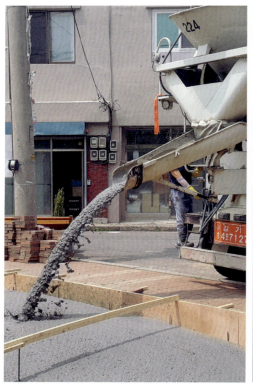 

Concrete pouring
After demolishing the existing pavilion, the site is cleared and graded. Formwork for the concrete foundation is installed with the help of a construction expert. After working with steel bars, 4 cubic meters of ready-mixed concrete is poured by a concrete mixer truck.

Leveling
A laser level kit on the tripod is used to adjust the level of the piers.

Placing concrete piers
After the concrete congeals, precast independent L-shaped concrete piers are arranged in the planned positions to support and stabilize the settling of the pavilion structure.

Anti-corrosive taping
Anti-corrosive taping is added between hardware connectors and lumbers to prevent corrosion from rotting.

Columns and rafters, in which three of the 2x6 components were alternately sandwiched and tightened with 75-millimeter screws, were fabricated as key structural sets. Then the sets were erected on top of the piers and connected with floor joists. The columns fixed to the piers were secured using a 90-millimeter stainless steel screw nail. An anti-corrosive tape, which was positioned between hardware connectors and lumbers, was also used to prevent corrosion and rotting. Zinc screws were used to tightly tie up the components.

After erecting the main structural frames, collar ties were tightly connected at the top of the gabled structure to prevent the roof from being lifted by the wind. The main column members were connected to the under-floor joists and beams, taking potential distortion of the structure into consideration. Given that the levels of floor joists vary due to different floor heights, the 2x6 double-layered components were used for the lower-floor joists, while the single components were utilized for the upper-floor joists. The double-layered components were joined with 75-millimeter stainless steel screw nails. A 38-millimeter stainless steel screw nail was used to fix the part where the columns and lower joists meet, using a diamond-shaped hurricane tie. Where the columns and upper joists meet, they were secured with the L-shaped skewed angle plate with a 38-millimeter stainless steel screw.

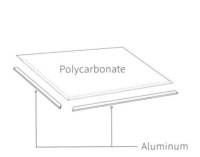

Polycarbonate end closure

After all components were cut, they were grouped and transported to the factory for ACQ preservative treatment for two weeks.

Deck floor joists

The spacing of each joist for the deck was no more than 400 millimeters wide to prevent distortion and load transfer, among other things. The 2x4 lumber was used for the floor deck. The components were secured with two 75-millimeter stainless steel screws at each meeting point to connect with the joists. The 2x4 lumbers were longitudinally stacked for low walls connected to the deck. The stacked lumbers were connected and screwed with steel-threaded rods with a diameter of 10 millimeters, and the nut for fixing the end of the bolt was used through silicon sealant to keep out moisture and fill seams. Approximately 2-millimeter-thick washers with an inner diameter of 10 millimeters and an outer diameter of 20 millimeters were fixed between the wall members to improve the durability of the lumber by securing air permeability.

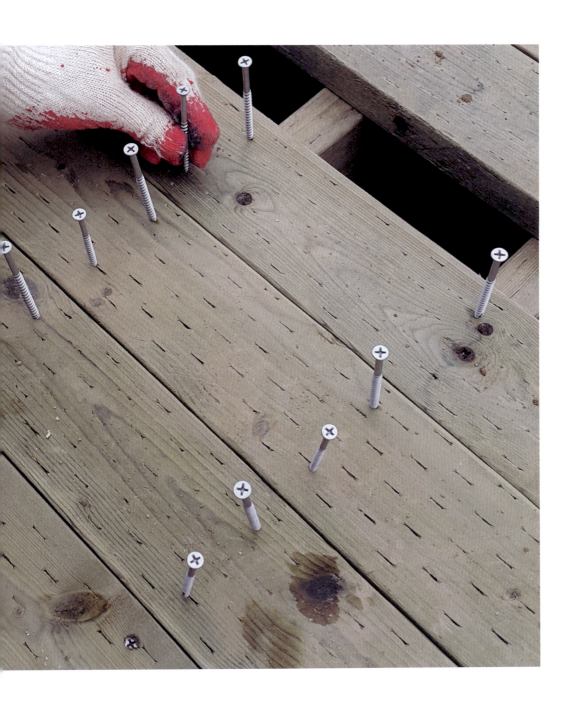

Roof structure and rainspout

Although grooves were cut in the gabled structures on the roof, purlins were used to tighten the structures and were fixed with screws. Polycarbonate sheets were used for roofing because they are lightweight (one-sixth of the weight of glass), durable, easy to maintain, and allow for cladding the larger roof with simple joints. The sheets were attached and fixed to the purlins using a 38-millimeter screw nail and sealed with silicon for waterproofing. The top of the roof, where two polycarbonate panels meet, was covered with L-shaped ridge zinc shingles.

Astonishing spatial effects were achieved by means of cladding with translucent polycarbonate sheets. The sheets work as a visual device that affects the transmission of light from the surrounding scene to the observers. The panels provide an opaque look, yet still let in ample light. An internal blinder was attached to control solar radiation to the pavilion. Rainspouts were installed on a slant in between three gabled roofs. The 130-millimeter-diameter plastic rainspouts have a gradient of 1:100 to efficiently drain rainwater to the rear of the pavilion.

Thirty graduate and undergraduate students participated in the final assembly of the components on-site with the help and technical support of Canada Wood Korea, which also supplied timber and other related supplies for the pavilion construction. The other supplementary donors were of great help. The previously abandoned and unattractive pavilion has been reclaimed, and the once dull and gloomy space has become a lively and friendly area for the residents. After its completion, the pavilion was donated to the residents of the Seoksu-dong Community in Anyang.

Interview
by Design Research and Innovation Lab, 2020

How did you decide on a site for each project, and was there any reason for choosing the site?

Jin-Ho Park: This series of works aimed to create pavilions was realized with funds raised from external sources. In some cases, we selected sites for communities by visiting and conducting surveys on these sites. In other cases, there were community organizations or people who directly contacted us for the construction of pavilions. There was also a case in which the local government office asked us to construct a pavilion in their suggested site. We focused on sites within communities that are alienated or abandoned. Among the proposed sites, we prioritized the most urgent, open-to-improvement, and public-interest sites.

What did it mean for a student to be involved in constructing pavilion structures to an actual scale?

Yongje Moon, student: Most of our works in the studio setting in school are limited to conceptual levels of designs. Hence, experiencing such designs being built in the field is difficult. By participating in these works, we were able to experience all processes, from conception to construction. It was a rare opportunity for us to learn the joinery details and experience the construction of the timber structure, and to watch the design's completion. I felt rewarded in constructing the structure from the perspective that this pavilion is a social contribution work for a shabby neighborhood.

You participated in the entire Seoksu Community Pavilion process from project planning to construction as a researcher. What was your experience?

Seoyeon Jeong, researcher: I was responsible for coordinating and communicating the opinions and ideas of participants in various groups, from planning to completing the design. Although developing the design and creating details after setting different concepts for each work were interesting, I experienced difficulty in planning the construction schedule and supplying the needed materials on the jobsite according to the initial plan. Safety during construction was my most important concern. Although the process was difficult, it was quite an experience participating in it.

Could you tell us about the children's reaction to the pavilion and what they usually use it for currently?

Nanny, Star of the Sea Children's Home: The structure and surrounding area have become a place for children to study or play outdoors while eating snacks during breaks. Before, there was no outdoor place for children to sit and play safely. On weekends, they often use the pavilion and the surrounding area for outdoor picnics. In the past, it was an empty and abandoned space, but it eventually became a preferred place where children can spend their extra time.

What has happened since the new structure has replaced the old pavilion?

Neighborhood resident, Anyang City: In the past, the pavilion floor was so low and uncomfortable to sit for long periods. At times, my back hurt as well. In the new pavilion, I can sit or lean on the right height of the pavilion, so my back hurts less. Moreover, the area used to have a dull atmosphere and was not an enjoyable place. With the new structure, the surrounding area of the pavilion has been transformed into a popular place visited by many elderly people nearby.

We heard that you were actively involved in the design and construction of some of the pavilions, and you were interested in the cross-sectional representation of timber components.

Youngsoo Kim, More Less Architects: As a participating architect, I am interested in pavilion designs that are relatively different from the ordinary. Hence, I like to experiment with various joinery details beyond that of the conventional timber structure. Moreover, I want to make a design that reveals the cross-section of the standard timber.

Your association helped the project team a lot, providing timbers, tools, and other materials and training participants in the basic knowledge of the timber-frame structure. How do you feel about the completed structures?

Canada Wood Korea: We were aware of the goal of the projects through various channels. If given the opportunity, then we are willing to donate and supply timbers and other materials for the projects. We used our network to provide the training program on the timber structure and construction method to the participants. We assessed that it was a meaningful activity for social contribution, so we were elated to be part of this undertaking. Moreover, the team's creative vision of developing new designs out of ordinary timber structure was phenomenal for us.

How did a large architectural firm get involved in the Bucket Pavilion project?

USUN: In recent years, the social responsibilities of professional architects have become an important trend, and our firm has provided free services to meet the needs of the socially disadvantaged or economically weak groups, consistent with the Korean Institute of Architects. As a professional architect from a large design firm, I only had a few opportunities to directly participate in community service activities such as this one. Even though it was minimal work, all timber components were hand-fabricated and assembled directly on-site. Therefore, such an experience was relatively different from designing large-scale buildings in the office.

Is there a reason you donated to the Courtyard Hideout project?

Christian Business Men's Connection: Our business group joined the project by mere chance. Someone in our group heard of this endeavor, in which a team at Inha University initiated an interesting social contribution project. In addition, there were calls for participation within our group. Unlike our typical one-shot donation activities every year to help people in need or childcare centers, the most significant attraction of this project is the team designs, constructs, and then donates the pavilions for needy communities. We thought that the entire process is worthwhile and meaningful.

Did you know what they were doing when there was a request from the research team and participants to use the equipment?

Gwacheon National Science Museum: They substantially knew our equipment list because we had several collaborations with the Inha University laboratory. One day, one of the researchers visited our laboratory to explain their goal and inquired about the possibility of using our equipment, such as the laser cutter and CNC milling machine. We were elated to help them because our laboratory is operated by a public institution and their activities were in line with the public interest and community development.

We heard that the Urban Regeneration Division at Anyang City was very interested in the Seoksu Community Pavilion project. Please explain how this project influenced the community.

Urban Regeneration Division: The project was closely related to our urban regeneration projects in Anyang City, so we enthusiastically collaborated with the team. We believe that this project became the first success story (or a leading model) of our city's public–private industry–academic collaboration project. We would like to express our gratitude to all participants for leaving behind an excellent precedent for Anyang City. Given that the project was conducted on public space for everyone's use, considering the opinions of various groups was definitely difficult. Some expressed complaints, while others were cooperative. Nevertheless, the project was completed successfully and impressively.

How did the Blooming Landscape project influence the department of the Seoul metropolitan city?

Landscape Planning Division: Although there were numerous requests from communities for similar projects, we are unable to accommodate all requests owing to our numerous tasks, budget limitations, and other reasons. In addition, it was not easy for the public domain to plan and implement similar projects, such as a public–private industry–academic collaboration. Given the success of this project, requests for similar endeavors have been coming in from nearby communities. At the city level, we will exert effort to continue such public–private industry–academic village linkage projects. I learned that the pavilion and the surrounding area are being actively used as a playground for children and resting area for the elderly. The community group recently stepped up and volunteered in maintaining activities around the pavilion, such as planting flowers, gardening, and cleaning.

Acknowledgments

Throughout each project, we had the opportunity to think about how small pavilions can inspire us to learn in a neighborhood and have pride in our community. Many have contributed to the production of each creative work and this book. We deeply appreciate and respect the valuable contributions of our partners and donors. Special thanks to the staff and students at Design Research and Innovation Laboratory (D-Lab) at the Department of Architecture at Inha University, Korea, who have been central to the production of each work. We are particularly thankful to Youngsoo Kim, Sejung Jung, and Yongje Moon for their valuable coordination on capturing and editing the overall book.

This book was also supported by Inha University Research Grant.

Published in Australia in 2025 by
The Images Publishing Group Pty Ltd
ABN 89 059 734 431

Offices

Melbourne
Waterman Business Centre
Suite 64, Level 2 UL40
1341 Dandenong Road
Chadstone, Victoria 3148
Australia
Tel: +61 3 8564 8122

New York
6 West 18th Street 4B
New York City, NY 10011
United States
Tel: +1 212 645 1111

Shanghai
6F, Building C, 838 Guangji Road
Hongkou District, Shanghai 200434
China
Tel: +86 021 31260822

books@imagespublishing.com
www.imagespublishing.com

Copyright © Dr Jin-Ho Park (text, photography and illustrations) 2025
The Images Publishing Group Reference Number: 1746

All rights reserved. Apart from any fair dealing for the purposes of private study, research, criticism or review as permitted under the Copyright Act, no part of this publication may be reproduced, stored in a retrieval system, or transmitted in any form by any means, electronic, mechanical, photocopying, recording or otherwise, without the written permission of the publisher.

A catalogue record for this book is available from the National Library of Australia

Title: Pavilions for Giving: Alternative Practice for Pro Bono Architecture
Author: Jin-Ho Park
ISBN: 9781875498376

This title was commissioned in IMAGES' Melbourne office and produced as follows: *Editorial* Rebecca Gross, Danielle Hampshire, Jeanette Wall, *Graphic design/Project management* Ryan Marshall, *Production* Nicole Boehringer

Printed on 140gsm Da Dong Woodfree paper (FSC®) in China by Artron Art Group

IMAGES has included on its website a page for special notices in relation to this and its other publications. Please visit www.imagespublishing.com

Every effort has been made to trace the original source of copyright material contained in this book. The publishers would be pleased to hear from copyright holders to rectify any errors or omissions.

The information and illustrations in this publication have been prepared and supplied by Jin-Ho Park and the contributors. While all reasonable efforts have been made to ensure accuracy, the publishers do not, under any circumstances, accept responsibility for errors, omissions and representations express or implied.